More than a collection of Puritan prayers, this book presents Puritan insights into God-centered, biblical spirituality in order to enrich our prayers. Donald McKim's brief but profound meditations are very helpful in the cultivation of what the Puritans called "a suitable frame of heart" to speak with our Father in heaven.

—**Joel R. Beeke**, President, Puritan Reformed Theological Seminary

The Bible describes the prayers of the saints as the incense that continually rises from the golden censer on the altar before the heavenly throne of the triune God. Donald McKim's *Everyday Prayer with the Puritans* provides the right kindling so that we can fan the embers of faith into a flame from which the incense of our prayers can rise into the heavenly holy of holies. He gives the church an excellent resource for both the joys and trials of life—Christ-focused prompts and prayers from our Puritan forebears from which we can all profit.

—**J. V. Fesko**, Harriett Barbour Professor of Systematic and Historical Theology, Reformed Theological Seminary, Jackson, Mississippi

A devotional that aims to help us pray with help from the Puritans should be enough to convince readers to "take up, read, and pray." But what I especially enjoyed about this book is how manageable it is: short devotions that strike the right balance between the Scriptures and the helpful theological ruminations from Dr. Donald McKim and the Puritans. If you struggle with prayer, you may find that this book is a helpful tool to make prayer a rewarding and soul-enriching daily habit. Even seasoned prayer-warriors will not fail to learn more about "familiar conversation with God" from this book.

—**Mark Jones**, Senior Minister, Faith Reformed Presbyterian Church, Vancouver

We all know prayer matters, but since we struggle, sometimes we either end up avoiding it or making it overly complicated. In this wonderful little devotional, Donald McKim draws on both his deep knowledge of the Puritans and his deep knowledge of God, offering us not only well-earned wisdom and sensible encouragement on prayer but also gentle questions to make sure we are making connections ourselves. His goal is not merely to teach us more about prayer but to help us actually to pray! McKim does not overwhelm but offers just enough to point us in the right direction and get us started. I hope it encourages you as it did me.

—**Kelly M. Kapic**, Professor of Theology, Covenant College

From the church fathers onward, theology was understood to be inseparable from worship and prayer. This connection has been eroded over the past few centuries. Don McKim's work is helping to repair this breach. Using his own reflections on the prayers and observations of major Puritan writers as a way to root good theology in Christian piety is a task he performs magnificently.

—**Robert Letham**, Professor of Systematic and Historical Theology, Union School of Theology

Dr. McKim offers a worthy companion to his earlier works encouraging everyday prayer. Between these covers, praying readers will find meditations on God's Word, pithy quotations from Puritans, and encouragements in the form of reflection questions and prayer points. Read this book on your knees and you will draw closer to the God of the patriarchs, the prophets, and other parents in the faith.

—**Chad Van Dixhoorn**, Professor of Church History, Westminster Theological Seminary

EVERYDAY PRAYER

with the

PURITANS

EVERYDAY PRAYER SERIES

Everyday Prayer with John Calvin
Everyday Prayer with the Reformers
Everyday Prayer with the Puritans

OTHER DEVOTIONAL WORKS BY DONALD K. McKIM

Advent: A Calendar of Devotions 2017
Breakfast with Barth: Daily Devotions
Coffee with Calvin: Daily Devotions
Conversations with Calvin: Daily Devotions
Living into Lent
Moments with Martin Luther: 95 Daily Devotions
Mornings with Bonhoeffer:
100 Reflections on the Christian Life
· *The Sanctuary for Lent 2017:*
Devotions with the Protestant Reformers

EVERYDAY PRAYER

with the

PURITANS

Donald K. McKim

P&R PUBLISHING
P.O. BOX 817 • PHILLIPSBURG • NEW JERSEY 08865-0817

Unless otherwise indicated, Scripture quotations are from New Revised Standard Version Bible, copyright © 1989 National Council of the Churches of Christ in the United States of America. Used by permission. All rights reserved worldwide.

Scripture quotations marked (KJV) are taken from the King James Version of the Bible.

Scripture quotations marked (RSV) from the Revised Standard Version of the Bible, copyright © 1946, 1952, and 1971 the Division of Christian Education of the National Council of the Churches of Christ in the United States of America. Used by permission. All rights reserved.

Printed in the United States of America

Library of Congress Cataloging-in-Publication Data

Names: McKim, Donald K., author.
Title: Everyday prayer with the Puritans / Donald K. McKim.
Description: Phillipsburg, New Jersey : P&R Publishing, [2021] | Summary:
   "The Puritans found God's goodness in day-to-day life; through
   meditative readings and reflective points, Donald McKim explores their
   teaching on prayer to inspire and inform your own devotions"-- Provided
   by publisher.
Identifiers: LCCN 2021008617 | ISBN 9781629957708 (hardcover) | ISBN
   9781629957715 (epub) | ISBN 9781629957722 (mobi)
Subjects: LCSH: Prayer--Christianity. | Prayer--Biblical teaching. |
   Puritans--Doctrines.
Classification: LCC BX9323 .M44 2021 | DDC 248.3/2--dc23
LC record available at https://lccn.loc.gov/2021008617

To Ford Trowbridge McKim

May he be blessed with a living Christian faith

Contents

Preface   11

A Note on Puritans   15

Using This Book   17

A Brief Prayer for the Morning   20

Kept from Being Overcome by Fears   21

Leave the Means to God   22

The Signature of Our Prayers   23

Mercies Come Thick   24

God's Glory and Our Good   25

Everything to God's Praise   26

A Prayer for the Evening   27

Commend All Things to God by Prayer   28

God's Sense out of Our Non-Sense   29

God Hears Our Tears   30

Hearts Fixed upon the Lord   31

Begin by Confessing Sins   32

An Ark in Christ   33

A Prayer before a Sermon   34

Prayer under Affliction   35

A Gracious Answer in Due Time   36

Confessing Our Sin   37

CONTENTS

Our Confused Prayers	38
The Lord of Our Times	39
An Absolute Promise	40
A Prayer after a Sermon	41
The Cause of Comfort	42
The Words of My Mouth	43
Prayer Is the Breath of Faith	44
The Chief Effect of Prayer	45
Your Everyday Prayer to God	46
Delayed but Not Denied	47
A Prayer of Adoration of God	48
Open Your Mouth to Be Filled	49
Prayer Lightens Afflictions	50
Observing God's Answers	51
Prayers Loaded with Mercy	52
The Two Wings of Our Souls	53
Prayer and God's Will	54
A Prayer for When We Are Dull in Prayer	55
Trying Your Affections	56
Praying for Right Direction	57
God Chooses the Best Time	58
To Wait on God	59
God's Promise—Our Hope	60
Graces in the Heart	61
A Prayer for Drawing Near to God	62
Even the Best Need Forgiveness	63
The Foundation of Our Works	64
God Takes Note and Listens to Us	65
Words and Heart	66
Begging God's Blessings for All	67

Amen!	68
A Prayer for Christian Living	69
God's Goodness in Teaching Us to Pray	70
Pray to Do God's Will	71
Practice What You Pray	72
In the Day of Temptation	73
Why God Desires Our Prayers	74
Praying and Living	75
A Prayer for All Times	76
A Gracious Calm in the Soul	77
Love to Neighbor and Love to God	78
By Prayer We Learn to Pray	79
Hallowed Be Thy Name	80
Pray for the Spirit	81
Praying for the Wicked	82
A Prayer for God's Help	83
Lifting the Heart to God	84
The Spirit Brings Things to Memory	85
The Breath of the New Creature	86
Difficulties Overcome by Prayer	87
Remarkable Providence Leads to Prayer	88
The Hand of the Soul	89
A Prayer That Christ Be Formed in Me	90
Pray with Confidence	91
Christ's Prayers Bring Acceptance of Ours	92
The Voice and Flame of Faith	93
For the Spirit of Illumination	94
Benefits of One Another's Prayers	95
The Power and Promise of God	96
A Prayer for the Spirit and Following Christ	97

Wait on God's Time	98
Talk Less and Pray More	99
Making Requests and Offering Thanks	100
Casting Our Care on the Lord	101
Effects of Our Prayers	102
Prayer and Thanks	103
A Prayer to Do God's Will	104
Pray Continually	105
Prayer Sweetens the Mercy	106
Pray for Others	107
Pray for the Saints of All Nations	108
With Holy Ardor and Desire	109
The Intercession of Christ in Heaven	110
A Prayer for the Church	111
Benefits of Christ Come through Prayer	112
Providence and Promises	113
True Prayer	114
A Stock of Prayer Going for Me	115
The Ears of God	116
A Heart Fit for Prayer	117
What God Wishes to Grant	118
A Prayer for Obtaining a Lively Hope	119
Index of Quotations	121
Writers	127
Selected Resources for Further Reflection	133

Preface

This book follows *Everyday Prayer with John Calvin* (P&R, 2019) and *Everyday Prayer with the Reformers* (P&R, 2020) to express the theology and practice of prayer as understood by sixteenth- and seventeenth-century English Puritans.

Puritans as a whole stood in the Reformed theological tradition of the Protestant Reformers and John Calvin (1509–1564). For them, prayer was a central reality in the Christian life. It is the means by which Christian believers can carry out Paul's instruction to the Philippians: "by prayer and supplication with thanksgiving let your requests be made known to God" (Phil. 4:6). This book presents quotations from these Puritans and my comments about their meaning and significance for Christian people who today live lives of faith and who pray.

My approach here is to provide a series of short devotional reflections on quotations from Puritan writers. Some prayers from Puritan writers are included as well. An identification of the writers of these quotations and prayers is provided at the end of the book.

As I have mentioned before, my vocational passion for providing books to introduce important theologians through comments on their quotations has grown over the years. My hope is that these books will open the treasures of theologians to those who are not familiar with their writings. The fact that their theological comments can nurture and benefit our Christian lives today shows that their theologies can live in the church and with Christian believers in the present time. Perhaps readers of the devotions will go on to explore more insights from these theologians. I hope so.

Prayer is a prime topic for theological reflection. Christian people pray. They pray in faith and move on toward understandings of prayer, based on Scripture and their experiences. Part of their experiences can be reflection on the nature of prayer as presented by others who have gone ahead in the faith and have provided theological thoughts about prayer.

My thanks again go to the fine folks at P&R Publishing for their interest and splendid help with this project. Dave Almack has been an insightful dialogue partner. Amanda Martin has been a wise and strong supporter, while Emily Etherton always provides perceptive suggestions. I would also like to thank my friend from college days, Bryce Craig, president of P&R Publishing, for his encouragement of these projects.

This book is dedicated to our grandson, Ford Trowbridge McKim. We welcomed Ford's birth soon after this manuscript was completed. We love him and pray for him to learn to pray and be a person of prayer throughout his life. May God bless Ford.

As always, my love and gratitude for my family runs deep. I could not do what I try to do without their love and support. LindaJo and I have been blessed by our family, and I am blessed by her love, care, forgiveness, and good humor in all our days. I cannot thank God enough for our lives together. Our sons and their families are wonderful blessings: Stephen and Caroline with our grandchildren, Maddie, Annie, Jack, and Ford; and Karl and Lauren are God's great gifts to us. They enrich us in so many ways, for which we give greatest praise and thanks to God.

My hope is that this book will introduce readers to Puritan writers who have significant and meaningful things to say about prayer. These writers can nurture and strengthen our faith as we pray by calling on God and thanking God from whom all blessings flow. May our faith grow and our devotion be deepened, and may we pray, "Hear my prayer, O God; give ear to the words of my mouth" (Ps. 54:2).

A Note on Puritans

W HILE defining sixteenth-century English "Puritanism" is a complicated issue, the theologians cited here are ones regarded as "Puritans" by historians of the period. In particular, most are found in the splendid work by Joel R. Beeke and Randall J. Pederson, *Meet the Puritans*.[1] The book ahead quotes only from English and Scottish—rather than American—Puritans.[2]

Puritanism arose during the reign of Queen Elizabeth I (1558–1603) as a movement within the established Church of England. It sought "reform" of the church, especially around elements of liturgy and worship (including vestments worn

1. Joel R. Beeke and Randall J. Pederson, *Meet the Puritans: With a Guide to Modern Reprints* (Grand Rapids: Reformation Heritage Books, 2006). For a thorough discussion of the complexities of defining Puritanism, see Randall J. Pederson, *Unity in Diversity: English Puritans and the Puritan Revolution, 1603–1689*, Brill's Series in Church History 68 (Boston: Brill, 2014). Also highly useful is the fine discussion and presentations in Joel R. Beeke and Mark Jones, *A Puritan Theology: Doctrine for Life* (Grand Rapids: Reformation Heritage Books, 2012).

2. Primary writings of Puritans can be found in electronic form at the Post-Reformation Digital Library: http://www.prdl.org/index.php. The most extensive digital collection of materials from this era is in Early English Books Online (EEBO). This source is available only through institutions that hold subscriptions to the collection, or through membership in the Renaissance Society of America (https://www.rsa.org/default.aspx). Also, texts can be found through the University of Michigan Library (https://quod.lib.umich.edu/e/eebogroup/) and at The Digital Puritan (http://digitalpuritan.net/).

by clergy). With varying degrees of intensity or "hotness," the movement was primarily "Reformed" or "Calvinist" in its theological outlook. It stressed a wedding of doctrine and life and a concern for holiness and piety in Christian living in devotion to Jesus Christ, so the nation and church could be renewed in all aspects. In all this, there was strong concern that church reform be based on the Word of God in Scripture.

There were variations in "the Puritan movement." These were especially among those who shared common goals about the importance of sound doctrine, lively piety, and personal and social renewal but disagreed on what polity or form of church government the national church should practice. The divisions were among proponents of the episcopal form of the Church of England; Presbyterians, who wanted the church to be led by "presbyters" or elders; and "Independents," who advocated a congregational form of church government in which individual congregations established their own leadership and autonomy without official connections to a hierarchy of leadership or other church bodies.

The Act of Uniformity was passed in 1662. It reasserted that the form of prayers in church worship, the administration of the sacraments, ordination by bishops, and other rites of the established church be practiced in the ways prescribed in *The Book of Common Prayer*. Those who did not adhere to this could not hold government office or positions in the church. Non-adherents were ejected from the Church of England and lost their church positions. They became known as "Dissenters"—many being called "Puritans"—and established their ministries in whatever ways possible. This period marked the establishment of Baptist, Congregationalist, and Presbyterian churches.

The Act of Toleration (1689), passed during the early reign of William and Mary, permitted these groups to exist and practice freedom of worship. But it also firmly sanctioned the established Church of England.

Using This Book

Tʜɪꜱ book introduces reflections of English Puritans on Christian prayer. Quotations from the Puritans are drawn from primary sources. The goal of this book is to present Puritans' understandings of prayer and show how these can nourish our Christian faith today. This book can be used for individual devotional reading as well as with groups.

The format of each devotion is the same. A Scripture passage is provided for initial reading. The context and emphases of the passage are mentioned in the text of the devotion. The order of the devotions in the book follows the biblical or canonical order of these Scripture passages. Some prayers of the Puritans are also given in the book.

The comments of the Puritans on prayer are provided, along with my reflections on their meaning and importance for contemporary Christians who pray.

Each devotion ends with either a prayer point or a reflection question. Prayer points suggest ways to use what has been described in a prayer. Reflection questions suggest further dimensions to what has been described, for reflection or group discussion.

I recommend the following approach:

1. *Read.* Read the Scripture passage at the top of each devotion. You can meditate on this Scripture before reading the devotion and keep it in mind as you read

the devotion. Each devotion is compact; every sentence is important. Contemplate each sentence as you read it.

2. *Meditate.* After reading the devotion, meditate on its instruction, asking questions such as the following:

- What has the Puritan conveyed here in the comments on prayer?
- In what ways can the church's life of prayer be deepened by the Puritan's insights?
- What do the Puritan's observations mean for my life of prayer?
- What new directions for prayer does this devotional call me to understand?
- What ongoing changes in the practices of my prayer life are pointed to by the Puritan's words?

3. *Pray.* Whether or not a specific prayer point appears at the end of the devotion, spend time in prayer reflecting on the Scripture passage, the Puritan's insights, and the comments in the devotion. Incorporate all you experience in your conversation with God in prayer.

4. *Act.* These insights about prayer may lead you to move into new directions or act in new ways in your life. Be open to the new dimensions of Christian living to which your prayers move you.

The title of each devotion expresses a main point of the devotion. As you read and reread these titles, recall what the devotion says and means to you.

If you keep a journal, incorporate insights about your encounter with prayer daily or at special times in the week. If you keep a prayer list, expand this to include what God's Spirit tells you through your devotional readings. These materials may be reviewed later and appropriated again for your life.

The devotions of the Puritans and their prayers can be read daily or upon occasion. I entrust this book to God's providence and the work of the Holy Spirit to be read and received in your life—whenever and wherever you read the devotions. Use the devotions prayerfully and in anticipation that God can—and will!—speak to you through them.

In some instances, I have modified spellings in quotations or provided definitions of archaic terms to enhance our understanding today. Citations are provided at the end of the book, indexed by author name and page number. Selected resources for further reflections are also provided to enable additional study of the Puritans.

O MERCIFUL Father, for Jesus Christ's sake, I beseech thee, forgive me all my known and secret sins, which in thought, word, or deed, I have committed against thy Divine majesty, and deliver me from all those judgments, which are due unto me for them. And sanctify my heart with Thy Holy Spirit, that I may henceforth lead a more godly and religious life.

And here, O Lord, I praise Thy holy name, for Thou hast refreshed me this night with moderate sleep and rest.

I beseech thee likewise defend me this day from all perils and dangers of body and soul. And to this end I commend myself, and all my actions unto Thy blessed protection and government, beseeching Thee, that whether I live or die, I may live and die to Thy glory, and the salvation of my poor soul, which Thou hast bought with Thy precious blood.

Bless me therefore, O Lord, in my going out and coming in; and grant that whatsoever I shall think, speak, or take in hand this day, may tend to the glory of thy name, the good of others, and the comfort of mine own conscience, when I shall come to make before Thee my last accounts.

Grant this, O heavenly Father, for Jesus Christ Thy Son's sake. Amen.

LEWIS BAYLY

Kept from Being Overcome by Fears

Genesis 8:1–5

T HE story of Noah and the ark in the midst of the great flood that covered the earth is dramatic. It shows God preserving God's people when they face the most devastating situations (see Gen. 6–9). God was faithful. Noah was told by God to build the ark. Now the people had only the security the ark provided. But their fears were overcome, and they came to safety.

God "remembered" Noah and his family and the animals in the ark. Through the winds that blew, "the waters gradually receded from the earth" (8:3). This did not happen all at once. But "at the end of one hundred fifty days the waters had abated."

William Gurnall applied this to our lives of prayer. He wrote that in prayer, we have "the bosom of a gracious God" to empty our "sorrowful heart into." "And though praying does not drain away all [our] fears," yet it keeps us—does it not—"from being over-flown" with fears, which we could not avoid without faith. Prayer offered in faith is our only hope for overcoming fears.

Praying may not unburden our souls of all our fears at once but "keeps the soul's head above the waves" and "gives a check to them that they abate (though by little and little)." Through faith we see the floodwaters of our lives subsiding as we continue to pray and keep on praying. Prayers offered in faith keep our heads "above the waves" and overcome our fears.

REFLECTION QUESTION: When have you experienced your fears being overcome as you maintained your prayers to God?

LEAVE THE MEANS TO GOD

Genesis 17:15–22

W HEN we pray, we tell God what we want. We may also tell God the ways we want God to answer our prayers! We are not the first to have these thoughts.

After Abraham was called and received God's covenant promise that in him "all the families of the earth shall be blessed" (Gen. 12:3), Abraham complained to God he was "childless" (15:2). Yet God promised Abraham's "very own issue shall be your heir" (15:4). After Ishmael was born to Abraham with Sarah's slave girl (16:3–4), God said Abraham's wife Sarah would bear a child to be the heir. But Abraham was concerned Sarah was too old and pleaded with God, "O that Ishmael might live in your sight!" (17:18). Abraham wanted to do it his way!

But we should leave the means of answering our prayers to God. We use the means God gives us, but, as John Preston urged, we should "keep our dependence" on God, and we should "leave it to him to use this, or that means, as it pleases him." Sometimes, said Preston, God may take away "that which we are about"; sometimes God "leaves us partly destitute, and finds a way of his own, that we might trust to him, and consider his power, and his wisdom, what he is able to do."

We pray to God, then "sit loose" on the ways God will answer our requests. God can do what God promises. We leave the means of answering our prayers . . . to God!

PRAYER POINT: In each of your prayers, pray for God to answer however God wills, and then be aware of the means God is using to answer your prayers.

THE SIGNATURE OF OUR PRAYERS

Genesis 24:42–49

T HE English Puritans strongly believed in the providence of God. They believed God ordained events in human history and human lives, leading and guiding them to fulfill the divine will. Prayer is a means by which God's purposes are known. Through prayer, persons are led to live out the will of God. Providence and prayer—prayer and providence—are linked together.

When Abraham's servant helped to find a wife for Isaac, at a well he prayed, "Let the young woman who comes out to draw, to whom I shall say, 'Please give me a little water from your jar to drink,' and who will say to me, 'Drink, and I will draw for your camels also'—let her be the woman whom the LORD has appointed for my master's son" (Gen. 24:43–44). Rebekah came to the well, and she responded exactly as the servant had prayed. Thus Rebekah and Isaac were married, and God's story of salvation continued.

John Flavel wrote, "Prayer honors Providence, and Providence honors Prayer." For "you have had the very Petitions you asked of him. Providences have borne the very signatures of your Prayers upon them. O how affectingly sweet are such mercies!"

Our prayers seek God's will and providence. When we pray, we will find God's providence leading us, and God's providence may show us what we had asked for in prayer—in ways we never expect! God's providence is the signature of our prayers. This is God's sweet mercy!

REFLECTION QUESTION: What are ways you have seen your prayers answered in what you believe to be God's providence leading and guiding you?

MERCIES COME THICK

1 Samuel 2:18–21

O NE feature of the Christian experience of prayer is what the Puritan theologian Thomas Goodwin called "overplus." By this he means that God may grant "above what we did ask." Sometimes we've received over and above what we directly prayed for in our petitions to God. This is a sign, Goodwin wrote, that God hears our prayers.

A biblical example is Hannah, mother of Samuel. She had prayed for a son (1 Sam. 1:10). God granted her prayer, Samuel was born, and she dedicated him to the Lord. Goodwin notes that Hannah had requested one male child, but God gave her three sons more and two daughters (see 2:21). This led Goodwin to say that "when prayers are answered, usually mercies come thick, they come tumbling in; the thing we prayed for comes not alone."

Have we thought of how "mercies come thick" to us when God does "far more than all we can ask or imagine" (Eph. 3:20)? God's mercies are so deep, wide, and embracing that we find ourselves giving thanks for the superabundance of what God has done in answering our prayers!

This shows us that God exceeds our expectations. When we pray, we never know the ways God will answer or the ways those ways may lead to many other things—which will be yet more mercies for us. "Mercies come thick"!

This should give us confidence when we pray—and hope that God's merciful blessings will surprise us with an "overplus" beyond our imaginings!

REFLECTION QUESTION: What does it mean to you that God's "mercies come thick" and that you receive more than that for which you have prayed?

GOD'S GLORY AND OUR GOOD

1 Chronicles 17:23–27

A KEY element in the Old Testament is God's covenant with David (see 2 Sam. 7:1–17; 1 Chron. 17). This covenant was in the form of God's promise to David that "the LORD will build you a house" (1 Chron. 17:10) and that God would establish the throne of David and his offspring "forever" (v. 14).

This covenantal promise led King David to go immediately to sit before God and to pray. He thanked God for being who God is—"there is no God besides you" (v. 20)—and for making Israel God's people (see v. 22). He said that God had revealed God would build David's house and "therefore your servant has found it possible to pray" (v. 25).

The great Puritan theologian William Ames wrote, "Our prayer is a necessary means for God's glory, and our good." David prayed, giving glory to God for the promise God made in covenant with David. God's goodness in the promise led David to pray. God's providential promise made David's prayer possible and enabled David to apprehend it by faith. So, wrote Ames, God's providence does "not make the true believers slothful, but doth more stir them up to prayer."

Through prayer we give glory to God and receive the benefits of God for our own good. Through prayer as conversation with God, we offer our praise and receive God's blessings. Prayer is the means by which our conversations with God occur and by which we speak to God and listen to God. Praise God!

PRAYER POINT: Pray that God will make you more faithful in prayer—both to speak to God and to listen to God.

EVERYTHING TO GOD'S PRAISE

1 Chronicles 29:10–13

A THEISTS are to be pitied because they have no one to praise or thank for blessings they receive! The opposite is true for Christians. We know the source of all our blessings and the One to whom our praise and thanksgiving is given. We acknowledge everything to God's praise. As Matthew Henry wrote, "Every bit we eat, and every drop we drink is mercy; every step we take, and every breath we draw, mercy. [These are] what we have reason to acknowledge with thankfulness to God's praise." This is comprehensive: we acknowledge all we eat and drink is of God's mercy. We give thanks in all things!

When Israel was presenting offerings for building the temple, King David blessed the Lord, giving thanks in his prayer for what God had done. He prayed, "Yours is the Kingdom, O LORD, and you are exalted as head above all" (1 Chron. 29:11). Then he added, "And now, our God, we give thanks to you and praise your glorious name" (v. 13). God is the Lord of all! God is to receive thanks and praise!

Our greatest purpose in life is acknowledging that everything—what we eat and drink and every breath—comes from God and praising God for this mercy. God is the source of all our blessings. Our prayers should ever and always be giving God all thanks as the "exalted head of all" and praising God's glorious name!

PRAYER POINT: Take special time in prayer to give praise and thanks to God for all blessings—even the most "common" things and all that you normally take for granted.

O MOST gracious God, and loving Father, who art about my bed, and knowest my down-lying, and my uprising, and art near unto all that call upon thee, in truth and sincerity; I wretched sinner do beseech thee, to look upon me with the eyes of thy mercy, and not to behold me as I am in myself. . . .

So, I beseech thee, sanctify unto me this night's rest and sleep, that I may enjoy the same as thy sweet blessing and benefit; that so this dull and wearied body of mine, being refreshed with moderate sleep and rest, I may be the better enabled to walk before thee, doing all such good work as thou has appointed, when it shall please thee by thy divine power to waken me the next morning.

And while I sleep, do thou, O Lord, who art the keeper of Israel, that neither slumbers nor sleeps, watch over me in thy holy providence, to protect me from all dangers, so that neither the evil angels of Satan, nor any wicked enemy, may have any power to do me any harm or evil. . . .

Hasten, O Father, the coming of our Lord Jesus Christ. Make me ever mindful of my last end, and of the reckoning that I am then to make unto thee; and in the meanwhile, care-ful so to follow Christ in the regeneration during this life, as that with Christ I may have a portion in the resurrection of the just, when this mortal life is ended. These graces, and all other blessings, which thou, O Father, knows to be requisite and necessary for me, I humbly beg and crave at thy hands, in the name and mediation of Jesus Christ thy Son. Amen.

LEWIS BAYLY

COMMEND ALL THINGS TO GOD BY PRAYER

Nehemiah 1:1–11

W HAT a task was ahead! Nehemiah, a Jew, lived among Jewish exiles in Babylon after they were deported in 587 BCE when Jerusalem was destroyed. Nehemiah sought and received permission to lead a group of Jews to rebuild the walls of Jerusalem.

When Nehemiah heard that those remaining in Jerusalem were in great trouble (see Neh. 1:3), he prayed for the people, asking God to remember the people whom God had redeemed "by your great power and your strong hand" (v. 10). He asked God to "be attentive to the prayer of your servant, and to the prayer of your servants" (v. 11). Nehemiah commended the task ahead to God, who was the people's Redeemer.

Arthur Hildersham commented, "They that are assured God by his providence ordereth all things, and the good success of every thing we take in hand depends upon his providence, must needs be careful to commend the success of every thing they take in hand unto God by prayer."

Nehemiah entrusted his coming service to God. We should also commend all things to God in prayer. For whatever we plan or do, we need to seek God's guidance and blessing. The results of all we do are in God's hands. So, in prayer, we should commit ourselves and all our actions to God's gracious providence. We trust God to lead and guide. As Nehemiah did, we ask God to help us glorify and serve God. We seek God's will. In prayer, commend all to God!

PRAYER POINT: Think of all you would like to do, are planning to do, and are doing. In prayer, commend each of these plans for God's service.

GOD'S SENSE OUT OF OUR NON-SENSE

Psalm 6:1–7

IT'S a good thing we don't have to have perfect prayers! Our grammar doesn't have to be correct, our thoughts don't have to be rightly formed, and we don't have to have a flawless list of things to say to God. Thomas Hall wrote, "It is not the loudness, or the length, or the neat expressions which take with God. . . . But it is the faith and sincerity of him that prays; poor broken prayers coming from a broken heart are of great worth in the sight of God."

Hall cites the Canaanite woman's prayer, "Lord, help me" (Matt. 15:25), and says, "Elijah's prayer was short and pithy" (see 1 Kings 18:36). He gives Psalm 6:3 as another example: "'My soul is sore vexed, but thou O Lord how long, viz. wilt thou delay to help me?' It is an abrupt broken speech, but God can pick sense out of our non-sense."

The psalmist prayed in the midst of his troubles. He was waiting for the Lord. He prayed from a broken heart, with bare faith in his cry for help.

But God hears and "can pick sense out of non-sense." No matter how or what we pray, God hears and helps, knowing what is deep in our hearts and healing our hearts as only God can do.

Thank God this is so! We can always pray from our hearts. God makes sense of it all.

PRAYER POINT: Listen to your heart and what is deepest within you. Pray short, heartfelt prayers, not trying to impress God but expressing your inmost feelings.

God Hears Our Tears

Psalm 6:8–10

O UR prayers can take a number of dimensions. There are the words we say or the thoughts we think. There are the desires of our hearts, and all our hearts are feeling when we pray. There are other dimensions too, like whether our prayers are spoken or silent or whether we plan our prayers or they rise spontaneously.

Beneath all these dimensions of prayer is the most important element: that we pray in faith. Faith is what matters most. Faith covers all parts of prayer, even when words may fail us.

Thomas Hall noted that "prayer is a work, of the heart, and not of the tongue, words are but the out-side of prayer, it is the heart's desire which God eyes and respects, and if thy affections fly aloft, though thy words do but creep, yet thy faith shall get what thy words cannot; yea if thou canst not speak, yet if thou canst weep, God will hear the voice of thy weeping; tears have a voice (Psalm 6:8), as well as words."

The writer of Psalm 6, in the midst of grave troubles, acknowledged that "the LORD has heard the sound of my weeping" (v. 8). In faith, we can weep before God, knowing God hears the voice of our tears. Prayer springs from the depths of our hearts, especially when our hearts are breaking.

Pray to God, even in the midst of tears and deep weeping.

REFLECTION QUESTIONS: Think of difficult and sad times in your life. Did you pray? Could you pray? Have you experienced the sense that God hears your tears, even when words fail?

Hearts Fixed upon the Lord

Psalm 25:1–3

P RAYER is an activity we practice in various times and different ways. Some expressions of our prayers are more intense
or focused than others. Sometimes we feel more "in the mood
to pray," while at other times it takes energy and willpower to
move us to prayer.

So it is important to realize that regardless of our time or
place or energy level for prayer, in prayer our hearts and minds
should be aimed to God. This is basic. But we can sometimes be
diverted from this truth.

Arthur Dent noted that when we pray to "Our Father who
art in heaven," we are directed toward God in heaven, and this
is where we are to be focused. He wrote, "Our hearts in prayer
must mount up into heaven, and be lifted up above all earthly
and frail things, how beautiful or goodly soever, and be wholly
fixed upon the Lord." He then cited Psalm 25:1: "To you, O LORD,
I lift up my soul." The psalmist began his prayer with his heart
and soul concentrated on the Lord.

In our fast-paced, technology-driven, action-packed cul-
ture, our times of prayer need to be oriented to God, rather than
on "all earthly and frail things"—no matter how interesting and
alluring those earthly things may be! Usually our attention is
drawn and diverted to dozens of things almost simultaneously.
In prayer, our attention is on God—listening to God and speaking to God. We are to be "wholly fixed upon the Lord."

PRAYER POINT: Make a conscious effort in your prayers
to keep your attention focused on God and what God is
saying as you express your prayers to God.

BEGIN BY CONFESSING SINS

Psalm 32:1–5

THERE are parts to our prayers. Often these are listed as Adoration, Confession, Thanksgiving, and Supplication (ACTS). Our prayers usually include all these, though they may tumble out in different orders.

In the prayers of the Puritans, the first main part is usually the confession of sins. The Puritans took sin very seriously—as does the Bible itself. Attention to our condition and relationship with God is a major—and primary—dimension of our prayers.

John Udall wrote that "it is necessary for God's people to begin their prayers to God with a free confession of their sins (Ps. 32:5; Dan. 9:5; Neh. 1:6). The reason is, because . . . else we obtain no forgiveness. . . . By the confession of our sins, we are the more humbled, and prepared the better to prayer."

We confess our sins up front so that we can be forgiven by God for breaking God's law, failing to do what we ought to do, and being unfaithful to God's will. After we confess our sins, Udall urges, we will be "more humbled, and prepared the better to prayer." In confession we recognize who God is and who we are—so that in humility, we may be forgiven and express our adoration, thanksgiving, and petitions to God. The psalmist recognized the need for confession of sins: "I acknowledged my sin to you, and I did not hide my iniquity" (Ps. 32:5).

We confess our sins and then repent—turn from sins and walk in ways pleasing to God. Begin by confessing sin . . .

PRAYER POINT: In your prayers, pay more attention to confessing your sins as an approach to God. Ask God for forgiveness and mercy.

An Ark in Christ

Psalm 32:6–7

W E all need help at some time. It may be for something relatively minor—or for something major. Various difficulties and distresses come upon us. When we face them, we need assistance—from beyond ourselves—to deal with dangers and agonies.

The psalmist recognized this need and urged, "Therefore let all who are faithful offer prayer to you; at a time of distress, the rush of mighty waters shall not reach them" (Ps. 32:6). In the dark days, pray to God. When you sense the coming of "mighty waters," pray!

David Dickson commented on this verse through the lens of God's provisions for us in Jesus Christ. He wrote, "It is possible, that a godly man may be in the midst of the waters of sore troubles, and yet these troubles not come near unto him, because God can furnish the man an Ark in Christ, whereby he shall swim above the deluge: and when God keepeth off trouble, that it proveth not hurtful."

Like Noah's ark, the "ark in Christ" can carry us through the deluge of the worst troubles so that we will ultimately be unhurt and safe in Christ.

We realize that as Christians we are not exempt from troubles or suffering. These difficulties may and will come to us. But God is with us, and in Jesus Christ we have a Savior. Christ saves us not only from sin but also from being completely drowned by "mighty waters."

REFLECTION QUESTIONS: Reflect on times when you have experienced your worst troubles and distresses. In what ways did you find God helping you by "the ark in Christ"?

Most merciful Father we humbly beseech thee to give every one of us grace to let these things sink deeply into our hearts. Bless we beseech thee our wills and affections with sanctified desires to entertain them, our memories with faithfulness to retain them, our minds with serious meditations to digest them, our hearts with fervency and prayer for thy blessings upon them, our lives with practice and piety to profit by them. . . .

Gracious Father, for this present holy business we have now in hand; we humbly beseech thee to let thy blessings be mightily upon thy Word at this time, that it may pierce and enter through to the dividing asunder of the soul and the spirit, of the joints and the marrow, and to discover the very thoughts and intents of the heart. Keep we pray thee out of our hearts and heads all troubles, cares, wanderings, humors, passions, prejudice, distractions, deadness or whatsoever . . . shall be suggested by the devil, or our own wicked hearts. So sanctify unto our souls this holy ordinance of thine, that we may handle and hear it with all feeling power and reverence as the Word of thee the true and ever-living God, and as that by which we must be judged at that last dreadful day. . . .

[All this] for the Lord Christ Jesus' sake: in whose glorious name and mediation we beg these and all other needful blessings. Amen.

Robert Bolton

PRAYER UNDER AFFLICTION

Psalm 34:11–22

TROUBLES. Suffering. Afflictions. We face these in life. Sometimes these are "of our own making." We sin; we face the consequences. Other times, they come upon us through no apparent fault of our own. "Undeserved suffering," we say. We are afflicted by what we have to endure.

We know, in the midst of it all, that we must keep focused on God. This is our only hope of enduring and emerging from whatever afflictions and difficulties with which we are confronted.

Vincent Alsop emphasized this when he wrote about "afflictive sorrows." Alsop saw these as a means of glorifying God. He cited James 5:13, which read in his translation, "If any man be afflicted let him pray." Prayer focuses us on God. What is the work of God in the midst of our afflictions? Said Alsop, "Prayer under affliction, witnesses that we believe our God to be good and gracious in it: that he can support us under it, can do us much good by it, and deliver us from it."

During afflictions, believe God continues to be good and gracious without fail. God will get us through the troubles by supporting us. In unexpected ways, God's good can come from our difficulties. Ultimately, God pulls us through, helping us in all circumstances. For "many are the afflictions of the righteous, but the LORD rescues them from them all" (Ps. 34:19).

God does not forsake us. God sees us through our afflictions as we pray . . . and continue to pray in the midst of whatever we face.

PRAYER POINT: Pray about whatever troubles, suffering, and afflictions you face. Focus on God's goodness, what God is doing in your life, and the hope of God's rescue.

A Gracious Answer in Due Time

Psalm 34:15–18

D OES God hear our prayers? We may wonder. Sometimes
it seems we pray—and pray and pray—and do not receive
any answers from God. In those times, our faith may flicker,
and we may need to reaffirm our faith that God does hear and
answer our prayers.

Arthur Hildersham wrote about what we need to remember: "We may be sure that as the Lord doth hear, and regard
every prayer we do make, so he will certainly give us a gracious
answer in due time. . . . No tender mother is so wakeful, and apt
to hear her infant when it cries; as the Lord is to hear his children whensoever they cry unto him (Ps. 34.15)."

Our relationship with God is a familial relationship. God
relates to us as a parent to a child. Yet God's love and care for
us surpasses even that of a parent for a child when God hears
the cries of God's child. God is more attentive to our cries and
prayers than even a "wakeful" mother!

The psalmist affirmed this by noting that "the eyes of the
LORD are on the righteous, and his ears are open to their cry"
(Ps. 34:15). God gives us "a gracious answer in due time," said
Hildersham. We may wait . . . and wait. . . . But God hears and
will answer at the time when God has willed. God's answer will
come, and it will be a gracious answer because God is gracious:
"the LORD is gracious and merciful" (Pss. 111:4; 145:8).

REFLECTION QUESTION: Think of those times when you
have prayed . . . and prayed more. Did God's "gracious
answer" come to you?

Confessing Our Sin

Psalm 38:17–22

THE whole human race has a problem: sin. According to the Bible, as understood in Christian theology, all persons are sinners: "All have sinned and fall short of the glory of God" (Rom. 3:23). None of us is in neutral; we are in reverse. We live for ourselves and not for the glory of God. We are alienated from God, guilty before the holy God. The psalmist said, "For your name's sake, O LORD, pardon my guilt, for it is great" (Ps. 25:11).

Confession of sin is part of Christian public worship and the Christian's everyday prayers. In confession, we acknowledge our sin and pray for God's forgiveness through Jesus Christ. We confess sins we have done and those things we have left undone—as theologians say, sins of commission and sins of omission.

Paul Baynes wrote about confessing sin: "Confession is an acknowledgement of our selves to be guilty, and worthily to have deserved God's wrath for our grievous offences; together with a free and humble bewailing of them before the Lord: such as are unknown to us in a general manner, but those which we do know (according to the nature of them) particularly." We say with the psalmist, "I confess my iniquity; I am sorry for my sin" (Ps. 38:18).

There is no other remedy for sin but confession. We cannot excuse or justify ourselves; we can only confess our sin. We confess our general sins and specific sins. Let us confess our sin.

PRAYER POINT: Take time to say a prayer that deals thoroughly with the confession of sin. Confess what you have done and left undone, both generally and specifically.

Our Confused Prayers

Psalm 38:9–12

G OD hears our prayers—whether spoken aloud, spoken in our hearts, or formed with longings and sighs without conscious words at all. As the psalmist said, "O Lord, all my longing is known to you; my sighing is not hidden from you" (Ps. 38:9).

This should give us great confidence when we pray, no matter what forms our prayers take. There are things deep within us, unformed in our minds, which are longings or sighs perhaps "too deep for words" (Rom. 8:26). In the jumble of all these, God hears.

Richard Sibbes wrote, "*My groanings are not hid from thee* [Ps. 38.9]; God can pick sense out of a confused prayer. These desires cry louder in his ears than thy sins. Sometimes a Christian hath such confused thoughts, he can say nothing, but as a child cries, 'O Father,' not able to shew what it needs, as Moses at the Red Sea."

Our prayers may be "confused"—we do not know what to pray for or how our prayers should be best constructed. Our prayers may be mightily "confused." As we direct all these to God, they are heard—even "louder" than our sins! Even when we can do no more than cry—and don't even know what we need—even then, like the baby Moses (see Ex. 2:6), our cries "melt" God "into compassion towards us," said Sibbes.

Trust God to hear and make sense of all your prayers!

PRAYER POINT: Pray to God, expressing the longings and groanings of your heart, even when these are not well-formed thoughts. Trust God to hear your confused prayers.

THE LORD OF OUR TIMES

Psalm 40:11–17

WHEN will God answer our prayers? This is a question we often ask. We pray and then want an answer—usually the sooner the better!

But we know we cannot demand that God answer our requests by a certain time. Our trust is that God will answer our prayers in God's time, which will be the best time. We know this, but we often have to remind ourselves of this. We do not want to wait. We identify with the psalmist: "You are my help and my deliverer; do not delay, O my God" (Ps. 40:17).

Thomas Brooks wrote, "The Lord doth not always time his answers to the swiftness of his people's expectations. He that is the God of our mercies, is the Lord of our times." God answers our prayers according to God's will and purposes. When answers to our prayers are delayed, we recognize God is the Lord of time. Our prayers will be answered according to God's will for our lives. Yet, as we wait in a "delay," we also realize "the Lord of our times" is also "the God of our mercies." God acts in mercy and love for us through God's answers to our prayers—even while we wait and pray for God not to delay and to "make haste to help me" (v. 13).

We can trust God, "the Lord of our times." And as we wait for God's help, we also trust "the God of our mercies." Thank God!

REFLECTION QUESTION: Reflect on what comfort and hope you have as you wait for God's answers, knowing God is Lord of our times and the God of our mercies. What does that hope look like in your life?

An Absolute Promise

Psalm 50:12–15

W E humans know about promises. We make promises. We receive promises. Promises come in different forms, and promises have different results. Sometimes promises are kept. Sometimes they are broken. We have to trust promises, but we know this is a venture of faith. No results are assured!

Unlike fallen humans, God does not break promises. God's promises are sure and can be fully trusted. God makes absolute promises; they will not fail.

The psalmist recorded a key text about God and prayer when God said, "Call on me in the day of trouble; I will deliver you, and you shall glorify me" (Ps. 50:15). God puts it clearly.

David Dickson said, "What more absolute promise can be made to a believing supplicant? . . . A believing supplicant shall not only be graciously answered to his petition, and so have cause of praising God; but also shall have grace in effect to praise God, 'And thou shalt glorify me.'" God's promise is absolute. Our petitions for help will be answered and, said Dickson, a believer "cannot possibly fall in any trouble out of which he shall not be delivered, but whatsoever evil come, he may be praying to God, yea he shall be delivered."

We can trust that our prayers are heard and that God will help—because this is God's absolute promise. When we experience this, by God's grace, we will praise and glorify God.

God promises and keeps promises. God's promises are reliable. God says, "Call on me!"

REFLECTION QUESTION: Think about your prayers to God for help. In what ways were you "delivered"?

O LORD our God, thou clearly sees and beholds from heaven, what hearts we now bring into thy glorious presence from the business of this day, how full of earthliness, deadness, listlessness, and unfitness to speak unto Thee. We pray Thee for Christ's sake to possess, quicken and sanctify them by thy blessed Spirit, that they may be ever feeling and fruitful in these holy exercises. Make us every day more and more wise, with all thy saints and elect children unto our eternal salvation in the right understanding, believing and obeying of thy blessed Word, and great mystery of godliness, in Jesus Christ our Lord. Amen.

ROBERT BOLTON

THE CAUSE OF COMFORT

Psalm 51:1–12

W HAT brings you comfort? We all like our "creaturely comforts"—we just define them differently and associate varying levels of financial costs with them!

What brings you the greatest comfort in your daily life? We can think of many things. But what is the greatest cause of comfort you experience?

What about the forgiveness of sins?

Arthur Hildersham appealed to Psalm 51 when he wrote, "That man that truly knows what sin is, accounts the pardon of his sin, to be sufficient ground, and cause of comfort in any distress." Our cause for comfort is to have our sin forgiven. The psalmist says, "Wash me thoroughly from my iniquity, and cleanse me from my sin" (Ps. 51:2).

Hildersham continued by saying, "David was now in great anguish of soul . . . he stood in great need of inward comfort, and that was his earnest desire, as you may see (vs. 8, 12). Make me to hear joy and gladness, restore to me the joy of thy salvation." This is great comfort!

Forgiveness of sins is our cause for comfort because this is the most serious matter we have to deal with in life. Our sins fracture our relationship with God. They set us going away from God's will toward pursuing our own wills, so our lives are directed into our paths instead of God's paths. Our sins should cause us anguish.

Day by day, we need the comfort of sin forgiven. We need to confess our sin and pray, "Restore to me the joy of your salvation"!

PRAYER POINT: Pray daily for God to forgive your sins. Thank God for this forgiveness.

THE WORDS OF MY MOUTH

Psalm 54:1–2

OUR prayers may be unuttered or expressed. We sometimes pray silently; other times we use our voice to pray to God. David Dickson pointed out the use of "the words of our mouth" when he wrote, "In fervent prayer, the very voice hath use, as with the supplicant to express his earnestness, and his faith in God, and to stir him up, and hold him fixed to his supplication; so with God also hath it use in regard it is an express invocation of him, and a sign of dependence upon him, and of expectation of a good answer from him; 'Hear my Prayer, O God, give ear unto the words of my mouth' (Ps. 54:2)."

Both in prayer and with God, one's voice can be important. Uttering our prayers aloud shows our earnestness in expressing what is within our hearts. Our verbal prayers give direct expression to our faith in God; they approach God seeking God's response. Prayers spoken can keep a focus on what is being requested from God.

With God, our verbal prayers directly invoke the Lord to hear the prayers we utter. Our words outwardly express our dependence on God. Our expressed prayers show we expect God's good answer to our prayers.

It is helpful in many ways to express our prayers out loud, even when we are alone. God hears. So we pray, "Hear my prayer, O God; give ear to the words of my mouth" (v. 2).

PRAYER POINT: For a period of time, pray out loud in your private prayers.

PRAYER IS THE BREATH OF FAITH

Psalm 61

WE sometimes use the phrase "the breath of life." This usually refers to ongoing life marked by and expressed in the act of breathing. Without the breath of life, only death is possible.

So too in the life of faith. Our faith "breathes" through prayer. If prayer is the breath of faith, then without prayer, faith dies. This was captured by William Gurnall's comment: "Prayer is the very breath of faith; stop a man's breath, and where is he then? . . . But for faith to live, and this breath of prayer to be quite cut off, is impossible."

In the prayers of Scripture, we see prayer as the expression of faith, just as breath is the expression of life. For example, the psalmist prays, "Hear my cry, O God; listen to my prayer" (Ps. 61:1). Then follows a psalm in which the writer invokes God (see vv. 1–2), trusts in God (see vv. 3–4), expresses certainty of being heard (see v. 5), intercedes for the king (see vv. 6–7), and concludes with an expression of the psalmist's confidence. Throughout, the deep faith of the psalmist is expressed in the prayer that comes to God in the form of a "cry" for God to "listen to my prayer."

When our prayer life wanes and our "breath" becomes sporadic, our spiritual lives are in danger. Physically, we cannot live without breathing. Spiritually, we cannot live in relationship with God without praying. Prayer is essential as the expression of faith. Faith must express itself in prayer.

PRAYER POINT: Prior to your prayer and at points throughout, breathe in and out, remembering that prayer is the breath of faith.

THE CHIEF EFFECT OF PRAYER

Psalm 65:1–4

P RAYING is not an option in the Christian life; it is an absolute necessity. Prayer is God's gift of grace, given to deepen our relationship with God through faith.

Ezekiel Hopkins commented that "God has commanded us to pray; not that he might be excited and moved by hearing the voice of our cries in prayer, to give unto us those mercies and blessings, which he himself was not resolved before hand to bestow upon us." Prayer is not twisting God's arm to award us what we request. We do not intend to change God's mind, to cajole and convince God to grant our prayers.

Instead, said Hopkins, there is another purpose for our prayers. We pray so "we our selves might be fitted and prepared to receive from him, what he is always ready and willing to confer upon us. He requires prayer from us . . . that we our selves might have our hearts raised and affected therewith. And therefore the chief effect of prayer being to affect our selves."

Our prayers change *us*. They focus us on God—who God is and what God wants to do for us—giving us love and blessings in Jesus Christ. Prayers raise our hearts to God, and this affects us too by bringing us into God's presence. We are always affected by a prayerful encounter with the living God who loves us and blesses us.

When we pray, we should all realize that we may never be the same again!

REFLECTION QUESTION: Do you remember times when your experience with prayer made direct and important changes in your life?

Your Everyday Prayer to God

Psalm 68:17–20

ENGLISH Puritans stressed that God "calls" people—to receive salvation and be disciples of Jesus Christ as well as to specific vocations through which they serve God in the world. These include work in society, in varying forms of service. Christians perceive their callings as ways they praise and serve God in all they do in their lives (see 1 Cor. 10:31; Col. 3:17).

Richard Baxter stressed that our labors in carrying out our callings should be undergirded by prayer. He wrote, "Make it your every day's prayer to God, before you go about the labors of your calling, that he would give you hearts to seek him in all, and would watch over you, and save you from ensnaring temptations, and remember you of himself, and give in somewhat of himself by his creatures, and sanctify them all to you."

Baxter's prescriptions are important today. Before we serve God each day, we should pray. This is most basic. In prayer, ask God to help you to seek God in all you do this day. Ask God to watch over and protect you. Pray for God to save you from temptations that can turn you away from serving God. Ask God to remember and look on you, that what you do may be pleasing to God and keep you in relationship with God. Ask God to make holy all you do.

Oh, "blessed be the Lord, who daily bears us up; God is our salvation"! (Ps. 68:19).

PRAYER POINT: Use the suggestions of Richard Baxter in your daily prayer to begin your day of serving God.

Delayed but Not Denied

Psalm 69:1–3

P RAYER is an act of faith in the God who is revealed in Holy
Scripture and known to us in Jesus Christ by the power of
the Holy Spirit.

The God of the Scriptures is a God who hears and answers
prayers. Prayer is God's gracious provision in bestowing a way
of fellowship with God as we converse with God—speaking to
God and listening to God.

Sometimes our prayers are not immediately answered. Our
faith is tested since we wait for God's response, which may seem
delayed or late by our timetable. The psalmist said, "My eyes
grow dim with waiting for my God" (Ps. 69:3).

But we should not despair or falter in our faith. As Thomas
Watson wrote, "God may hear us when we do not hear from
him; as soon as prayer is made God hears it, though he doth
not presently answer. A friend may receive our letter, though he
doth not presently send us an answer of it. . . . God may delay
prayer, and yet not deny."

Our communication with God occurs when prayer is
offered. This is instantaneous. But God may not answer right
away. On a human level, it may take us some time to answer an
email or a letter from a friend. On a divine level, God may delay
in answering our prayer, but this does not mean God will deny
answering our prayer. God's timing is not always our own.

We pray in faith. We wait for God in faith.

REFLECTION QUESTION: What does it contribute to your
prayer life to believe that God's answers to our prayers
may be delayed but not denied?

O Lord our God,

Thou art worthy, O Lord, to receive blessing, and honor, and glory, and power; for thou hast created all things, and for thy pleasure, and for thy praise, they are and were created. We worship him that made the heaven and the earth, the sea, and the fountains of waters; who spoke and it was done, who commanded and it stood fast; who said, Let there be light, and there was light; Let there be a firmament, and he made the firmament; and he made all very good; and they continue this day according to his ordinance; for all are his servants. . . .

Thou art good, and thy mercy endures for ever. Thy loving-kindness is great toward us, and thy truth endureth to all generations. Thou hast proclaimed thy name; the Lord, the Lord God, merciful and gracious, slow to anger, abundant in goodness and truth, keeping mercy for thousands, forgiving iniquity, transgression, and sin. And this name of thine is our strong tower. Thou art good and does good; good to all, and thy tender mercy is over all thy works. . . .

We are thine, save us, for we seek thy precepts: It is thine own, Lord, that we give thee, and that which cometh of thy hand. Amen.

MATTHEW HENRY

OPEN YOUR MOUTH TO BE FILLED

Psalm 81:6–10

G OD is faithful to God's people. God calls and provides for those related to God in faith. They pray to God and rely on God for their lives of service to their Lord. God's self-description emphasizes this relationship: "I am the LORD your God" (Ex. 6:7; 20:2).

Since God provides and "stays with" the people, God's people ought to "stay with" their Lord by faith, not being discouraged, especially in prayer. Nathaniel Vincent put it this way: "The Lord perseveres in attending and encouraging, therefore we should persevere in praying. His eye is continually upon his people; eye, and ear, and heart, and hand are all open, and if we open our mouths wide we shall be filled."

Vincent's emphasis is on God's people praying . . . and continuing to pray. Through all the groanings, doubts, discouragements, and delays, God's people persevere in praying in faith. God's constant watching and caring continues. God's heart and hands are "all open," said Vincent. Then he echoes the psalmist: "I am the LORD your God, who brought you up out of the land of Egypt. Open your mouth wide and I will fill it (Ps. 81:10)."

Will we be open to being filled by God? God gives us blessings we may receive—if we will. We may not be open to being filled. When we look to ourselves, seeking our own ways, we "close our mouths," and our lives are empty. When we look to God, God's overflowing love and mercy are lavished upon us; by God's grace, we may be filled!

PRAYER POINT: Pray to be open to receiving answers to prayer and blessings from God.

PRAYER LIGHTENS AFFLICTIONS
Psalm 94:16–19

P SALM 94 affirms God's power in the midst of the afflictions of God's people. In the face of troubles, God helps the righteous. No matter how severe the difficulties, God's steadfast love (covenant love) holds up God's people (see Ps. 94:18). "When the cares of my heart are many," said the psalmist, "your consolations cheer my soul" (v. 19). The psalmist prays in thankfulness for God's timely and continuing interventions and blessings in his life.

In the midst of afflictions, the psalmist prays and thanks God. Do we?

When we face the difficulties of life—whatever they are—we need all the help we can get. Our best help comes from God. We receive God's help through prayer as we share with God the afflictions we feel.

Edward Reynolds wrote that we are eased when we realize "prayer lightens affliction where it does not remove it. . . . In prayer we must seek the face of God; His favor to comfort us, and his Counsel to direct us."

Our prayers help us through afflictions. Prayer is not an automatic fix for troubles, a way to get them removed. But prayer assures us of God's steadfast love that helps us to move through the problems we face. In prayer, we seek God's presence. We find God's favor—the love that comforts us in all ways. We seek God's counsel to direct and guide us so that we will know what ways God wants us to follow as we are sustained by God's loving mercy.

PRAYER POINT: Lay out all your afflictions and troubles before God in prayer. Realize you are in God's presence. God's love holds you in comfort, and God will show you the way to follow.

Observing God's Answers

Psalm 116:1–2

W E make our prayers to God. We believe God answers our prayers. But do we always take time and seek the wisdom to recognize God's answers to our prayers?

Sometimes we see what seem to be "natural events" as just that—natural events. In reality, they may be God's way or means of answering our prayers. Some things we pray about, perhaps in fear or dread, never happen. Those are God's answers to our prayers, if only we will recognize them as such. Or we may forget our prayers about something, only to realize—much later—that our prayers were answered. We did not recognize it at the time and then forgot about it.

Thomas Goodwin wrote, "If you observe not his answers, how shall you bless God and return thanks to him for hearing your prayers?" We need to watch for God's answers to our prayers. God's answers, when we see them, strengthen our faith and are a sign of God's love and care for us. The psalmist said, "I love the LORD, because he has heard my voice and my supplications. Because he inclined his ear to me, therefore I will call on him as long as I live" (Ps. 116:1–2). Then the psalmist praises and thanks God throughout the remainder of the psalm. We need to observe God's answers to our prayers so that we can "bless God and return thanks" to God! We watch, observe, and recollect God's answers to our prayers so thanksgiving can be given to the Lord.

REFLECTION QUESTIONS: Do you observe God's answers to your prayers? The Puritans kept written records of the answers to their prayers. Would this be a valuable practice for you?

Prayers Loaded with Mercy

Psalm 116:1–7

WATCHING for God's answers to our prayers is a "necessary ingredient" said Nathaniel Vincent. Why? Because, wrote Vincent, "the more watchful you are in prayer, the more experimentally will you understand the loving kindness of the Lord; you shall find that he deals bountifully." He cites the psalmist: "Return, O my soul, to your rest, for the LORD has dealt bountifully with you" (Ps. 116:7). When we receive the answers to our prayers, we experience for ourselves how God has blessed us and given us grace and mercy.

Vincent went on to write that "God is certainly willing to give; they that watch in prayer, take notice what they receive; and great joy it is to behold the prayers, which as messengers we dispatched to Heaven, return loaded with mercy." We express our prayers to God—our petitions and supplications. God answers our prayers. When we experience God's answers, we find they are "loaded with mercy"—because "our God is merciful" (v. 5)! God is "gracious" (v. 5), hearing our voice and supplications (see v. 1), saving us from "distress and anguish" (v. 3), and dealing "bountifully" with us (v. 7). God gives us grace and mercy we do not deserve—but for which we give God praise and thanksgiving!

We can rest in God because God hears our prayers and answers them. God gives us mercy upon mercy, enabling us to experience the fullness of God's love for us. No wonder it is necessary for us to watch for God's answers!

REFLECTION QUESTION: Think of God's answers to your prayers. How were God's answers "loaded with mercy"?

THE TWO WINGS OF OUR SOULS

Psalm 119:25–27

WE often say prayer is speaking to God and listening to God. There is a dialogue in prayer. We speak to God of our petitions and desires and then listen, in stillness, to what God leads us to reflect and meditate on, by the power of the Holy Spirit.

John Downame said that the first service "we are to offer unto God consists in prayer and meditation, which are the two wings of our souls, whereby they soar aloft into heaven, and there enjoy the presence of God."

In the speaking and listening of prayer and meditation—"the two wings of our souls"—we are brought into the presence of God. This is a unique experience in our lives. Through prayer we offer praise and thanksgiving to God, telling God what is deep in our hearts. Through meditation we listen to God to sense and know what God desires of us and contemplate God's wondrous works. The psalmist said, "When I told of my ways, you answered me; teach me your statutes. Make me understand the way of your precepts, and I will meditate on your wondrous works" (Ps. 119:26–27). In our conversations with God, we speak and listen, glorifying God, increasing our communion with God, having our faith strengthened and our hearts enlarged with love and thanksgiving.

The "two wings of our souls," prayer and meditation, bring us into the presence of the living God.

> **PRAYER POINT:** Pray to God. Then spend time meditating on God's works and your experience in speaking to and listening to God.

Prayer and God's Will

Psalm 119:33–40

THE Puritans were great believers in God's will being the source of all things. God is the Lord of heaven and earth, of time and history.

God's will embraces all things, including the lives of all people. As believers, we pray to God, and we believe our prayers are important—heard and answered by God.

So what is the relationship between God's decrees and human prayer?

Thomas Taylor addressed this with a question: "But has not God decreed unchangeably what to do, whom he will teach, whom not? So as our prayer or not prayer can never alter his decree?" Taylor then answered, "God hath decreed as well how to do things, as what he will do: and therefore God's decree takes not away prayer, but establishes it." In other words, God decrees not only what occurs but the means by which those things will occur, and prayer is a means God uses to establish what God wills.

So our prayers are important because they are used by God to carry out the divine purposes. Prayer is part of the process of God's fulfilling God's will. God decrees what to do and how it will be done. Prayer is a means God uses and is part of God's decree itself. So prayer is vitally important! The psalmist prayed the following: "Teach me, O LORD, the way of your statutes, and I will observe it to the end" (Ps. 119:33). We pray to follow God's statutes—which include our prayers!

REFLECTION QUESTION: Reflect on how important prayer is and how much freedom we have in prayer to see our prayers themselves as part of God's divine will. Has recognizing this changed your attitude toward prayer?

O LORD God, most merciful Father, according to thy commandment, in mine afflictions, and necessities, I seek to thee for succor by continual prayer and calling upon thy name. . . .

Strengthen me by thy holy Spirit, that I may still persevere and continue in prayer, and with longing desires patiently wait for thee O Lord, being assured that although it appear not, yet thou art always present with me, and hear my sighs and complaints, and will when thou seest thy time declare thy self manifestly in the renewing my heart with spiritual joy: stir up O Lord my dull and sluggish nature, to call upon thee continually, appointing thee neither time, nor the means of my deliverance, but leaving all to thy good will and pleasure. . . .

I feel myself (O Lord) oftentimes very unwilling to pray, for that I do not fully perceive my prayers to be heard, but do go on still languishing in my sorrows, as though thou hadst no care of me. But this my dullness, I beseech thee, O merciful Father, pardon in me, and grant that I may be raised up to pray for aid and relief of thee continually, although I should see no sign of favor, yet that I may continue still, with the faithful woman of Canaan, and never cease in heart, mind, and mouth, till thou grant my requests at thine appointed time, when thou knowest it shall be most for my behalf, and for thy glory.

And that when thou shalt mercifully look upon me to deliver me: I may then fully with my whole heart acknowledge thy goodness toward me, and let it never stir out of my heart, but continue thankful for the same all the days of my life, whereby thy glory in me may be declared, and my soul relieved through Christ my Lord and Savior, Amen.

EDWARD DERING

TRYING YOUR AFFECTIONS

Psalm 139:19–24

W E have great freedom in prayer to express the desires of our hearts. Yet we must always recognize that our freedom should be directed toward requests we believe to be in accordance with God's will. Our "affections in prayer" should be ones God would want to bless and prosper. As Richard Baxter put it, "Try your affections in prayer before God, whether they be such as you dare boldly pray God either to increase or continue and bless; and whether they be such as conscience hath no quarrel against."

We cannot ask God to bless attitudes or actions that we know to be against who God is and what God wants for the world, the church, and us. Our prayers should not be made randomly or willy-nilly—putting forth whatever happens to cross our minds at prayer time. Our petitions and prayers should express the affections of our hearts, which should be in line with what we can believe God wills and desires. Baxter notes that our affections should be ones our "conscience has no quarrel against." Are we praying with a clear conscience with what we ask? We should pray with the psalmist, "Search me, O God, and know my heart; test me and know my thoughts" (Ps. 139:22).

Trying our affections gives value to prayer because we are presenting what we honestly believe to be requests that God can honor as being in accord with God's will. Always, we are to pray "lead me in the way everlasting" (v. 24).

PRAYER POINT: Examine the things for which you usually pray. Are they all things you believe to be pleasing in God's sight? Make any adjustments in accord with your conscience and God's Word.

PRAYING FOR RIGHT DIRECTION

Isaiah 30:19–22

SOMETIMES we don't know what to do or which way to turn. Different options may compete for our decision. What if we are doubtful or uncertain about what God wants us to be or do? Even when we have examined all the options, no way may open up as the clear path for us to follow.

In these times, we need to pray. To pray is to seek to align ourselves with God's purposes and how God wants us to live. It is to seek a communion with God in speaking and hearing that is not found in any other place or in any other way. Prayer is crucial to our decision making.

In times like these, we need to pray for God to direct us in the right way and course, the right direction. As Thomas Gouge put it, "Prayer being the means sanctified by God for the obtaining of every good thing, be earnest with God in prayer, that he would direct thee in the right way and course; that he would cause thee to hear a voice behind thee, saying, This is the way, walk in it." Gouge was quoting the word given to Isaiah about God's promise for the future (see Isa. 30:21).

By God's grace, prayer helps us to be led in right directions. Prayer opens us in willingness to follow God's Spirit, who leads us in God's ways. Pray for right direction. Hear God's voice . . . follow it . . . and walk in God's way!

PRAYER POINT: If you need to find God's direction, pray about it. If you think you know God's way and course for you, pray about this to be sure it is God's will.

GOD CHOOSES THE BEST TIME

Isaiah 49:8–12

W E know our own lives, from our own perspectives. God knows our lives, from God's perspective. We should be glad that there is One who knows us beyond ourselves and who knows us fully. After all, God is our Creator!

When it comes to answering prayers, we should be glad it is God to whom we pray . . . and not we ourselves. For God hears our prayers and answers our prayers in God's own time—not our time. God's chooses the best time to answer our prayers, for which we should be immensely grateful!

Thomas Goodwin pointed out that "God considers all times of thy life, and still chooses the best and fittest to answer thy prayers in, 'In an acceptable time have I heard thee' (Isaiah 49:8). . . . So accordingly God answers in the best and most acceptable time to us. . . . He is a wise God that knows the fittest times and seasons, wherein to show kindness, and to deal forth his favours in."

In anticipation of God's future actions with Israel, God said, "In a time of favor I have answered you" (Isa. 49:8), as Goodwin quoted. God's answers to our prayers now are God's favor to us, and they come at the best time for us. God is all-wise and knows our lives infinitely better than we do. So we should be glad to trust God's timing for the answers to our prayers! But do we trust "God's time" as our "best time" for receiving God's answers to our prayers? Let's trust!

> **REFLECTION QUESTION:** Do you find it easy or difficult to trust God's time to be the best time for receiving God's answers to our prayers?

To Wait on God

Lamentations 3:21–26

WHEN we hear the phrase "to wait on God," we probably initially think of waiting for God to answer our prayers. But "to wait on God" can also point us toward a continual sense of living in the presence of God. We wait—and await!—what God is doing and saying to us through various means. As we read Scripture, pray, and converse with others, we experience things that happen to us. We wonder if these are ways God's presence is being made known to us. In the broadest sense, we "wait on God" for our salvation—living out the salvation that has come to us in the life, death, and resurrection of Jesus Christ. The poet in Lamentations wrote, "The LORD is good to those who wait for him. . . . It is good that one should wait quietly for the salvation of the LORD" (Lam. 3:25, 26).

Matthew Henry wrote, "It is our duty in the morning to speak to him in solemn prayer; but have we then done with him for all day? No, we must still be waiting on him, as one to whom we stand very nearly related, and very strongly obliged. To wait on God is to live a life of desire towards him, delight in him, dependence on him, and devotedness to him."

Desire, delight, dependence, and devotedness to God. Do we "wait on God" in these ways?

PRAYER POINT: Write a special prayer to God asking for help to "wait on God" by affirming your desire, delight, dependence, and devotedness to God. Pray this prayer often.

GOD'S PROMISE—OUR HOPE

Lamentations 3:40–41

IN the midst of devastating tragedies and sorrow, the poet of Lamentations seeks hope. All around, enemies, destruction, and sin abound. Things are as discouraging as they can be.

Then, in Lamentations 3, hope comes! God's steadfast love endures, even in the midst of great suffering.

The poet takes hope, urging a "return to the LORD" (v. 40) and praying, "Let us lift up our hearts as well as our hands to God in heaven" (v. 41). Only "God in heaven" can give and sustain hope when all else fails. So, John Udall wrote, "the prayer of the faithful must never rest upon anything in this world, but look unto the mighty God, the author of all things. The reason is, because faith reaches above reason, or things that are seen. The use is to teach us, not to measure our hope when we pray, by our own worthiness or understanding, but by the promise of God, grounded upon his power and truth."

To the eye of reason, all hope seems gone. To pray to "God in heaven" is to look beyond ourselves—our "own worthiness or understanding"—and to measure hope by the promise of God, which is grounded in God's power and truth. God's promise is our hope—nothing else! Only God's promise of being with us and loving us can give us the hope we need, no matter how dark the days. We focus on "the mighty God," not ourselves. God's promises are sure and will not fail!

PRAYER POINT: Focus your prayer on the hope of God's promise—fulfilled in Jesus Christ. Look beyond your current situation to the sure, certain, and everlasting promise of God.

GRACES IN THE HEART

Ezekiel 37:11–14

RICHARD Baxter spoke of the habits the Holy Spirit brings as the Spirit illumines and sanctifies us, helping us to grow in the grace of God. He listed love to God and goodness, thankfulness for mercy, faith in Christ and the life to come, hatred of sin, and leading us to a "constant habit of prayer."

Then Baxter wrote that "prayer is nothing but the expression with the tongue of these Graces in the heart: So that the Spirit of Sanctification is thereby a Spirit of Adoption and of Supplication. And he that hath freedom of utterance can speak that which God's Spirit hath put into his very heart. . . . This is the Spirit's principal help."

The Spirit of God is fulfilling the promise to the prophet Ezekiel when God said, "I will put my spirit within you, and you shall live" (Ezek. 37:14). When God's Spirit is within us, we break forth in prayer as an expression of God's grace and graces in our hearts.

The Spirit of God enables us to pray as our love for God increases and we seek God's will. We have a spirit of thankfulness for God's mercy to us, in Jesus Christ, as we have faith in him. We seek to turn from sin and anticipate the hope of eternal life. These graces and others are established within us by the Holy Spirit. They bless us. Our prayers break forth in outward expression of the Spirit's help.

May we always respond to the Spirit's work in our lives by praying!

> **PRAYER POINT:** Think of all the Spirit has done and is doing in your heart and life. Pray in great praise and thankfulness for the Spirit's work.

O God . . .

Thou hast commanded us to pray always, with all prayer and supplication with thanksgiving, and to watch thereunto with all perseverance and supplication for all saints; to continue in prayer; and in every thing by prayer and supplication to make our requests known to God.

Thou hast directed us to ask, and seek, and knock, and hast promised that we shall receive, we shall find, and it shall be opened to us.

Thou hast appointed us a great High Priest, in whose name we may come boldly to the throne of grace, that we may find mercy and grace to help in time of need. . . .

Thou art he that hears prayer, and therefore unto thee shall all flesh come.

Thou sayest, "Seek ye my face," and our hearts answer, Thy face, Lord, will we seek. For should not a people seek unto their God? Whither shall we go but to thee? Thou hast the words of eternal life. Amen.

MATTHEW HENRY

EVEN THE BEST NEED FORGIVENESS

Daniel 9:15–19

W E hear about our need for forgiveness of our sins. Church services mention this, many including a prayer of confession in their weekly worship services. Prayers from the pulpit mention this—as do the Scriptures, of course! The need for forgiveness of sins is part of the message of the Christian faith.

Do we really need forgiveness? Most of us think we are pretty decent people, not committing big-time sins but in our daily lives acting kind to others, helping as we can, and being pleasant folks.

But there are deeper issues: attitudes of selfishness, pride, anger. We may sin by subtly manipulating others, walking away from the needy, or showing apathy for biblical emphases such as justice, peace, and love. For all these, we need forgiveness.

William Lyford wrote that when we pray "forgive us our debts" (Matt. 6:12), we pray that "God would give to every one of us faith and repentance, by which we may be accepted into his favor, in, and for Christ's sake; having all our sins freely and fully done away by him. . . . The best have need every day to pray forgive us our sins." We need to pray with Daniel, "O Lord, hear; O Lord, forgive" (Dan. 9:19).

Even "the best," said Lyford, need forgiveness. We *need* to examine ourselves, recognizing that no matter how "virtuous" or "pure" we think we are, we always need forgiveness of our sin. "O Lord, forgive."

PRAYER POINT: Think as thoroughly and honestly as you can about ways you have fallen short of who God wants you to be, ways you have offended God and not loved others. Ask for forgiveness.

THE FOUNDATION OF OUR WORKS

Zechariah 12:10–14

I T is easy to be "weary in well-doing" (Gal. 6:9 RSV). If we live an active life of Christian faith and seek to express our faith by doing things that please God and serve others (called "good works"), it is possible to become weary, burn out, or suffer a power failure of the spirit.

We know that what we do in service to God and others is not maintained by our own stamina or powers of perseverance. If we think we provide all the momentum and impetus for our works of serving, we are mistaken and "weariness in well-doing" can set in.

Instead, we need to hear the counsel of Edward Leigh: "[God] commands us to pray and make known our wants to him, and promises to 'pour upon us the spirit of grace and supplication' [Zech. 12:10]. God's promises are the foundation of all our performances. For we by working do not cause him to fulfill his promises, but he by promising doth enable us to perform our works."

God's promise to Zechariah was that we should pray and God will "pour out . . . a spirit of compassion and supplication" (Zech. 12:10). God provides the spirit—of compassion, grace, supplication—and we receive. So, Leigh notes, our works do not cause God to fulfill divine promises. Instead, God's promise enables us to do what God calls us to do in works of service. The foundation of our works is God's word of promise, not our own efforts. Pray and receive God's Spirit!

REFLECTION QUESTION: Reflect on ways you serve and what you do to express your faith. In what ways are you conscious of God's promises as being the foundation of all you do?

God Takes Note and Listens to Us

Malachi 3:16–18

W HEN our prayers are not answered according to our timetables, we may get discouraged. This is common among those who pray.

So it's important to remember that God's timing in answering our prayers is the best and that as we wait for God to answer, we should not think God has forgotten us or missed hearing our prayers.

Paul Baynes wrote that "God does on so good occasions, delay us in our suits [meeting our desires]. And let us be sure of this that he that bottles up our tears, files up our prayers, putting them on record before him." Then Baynes quoted the prophet Malachi: "The LORD took note and listened, and a book of remembrance was written before him of those who revered the LORD and thought on his name" (Mal. 3:16).

God takes note and listens to us when we pray. God "bottles up our tears," wrote Baynes, reminding us of the psalmist: "You have kept count of my tossings; put my tears in your bottle. Are they not in your record?" (Ps. 56:8). Our prayers are not launched into empty space. They are heard and stand before God, who will answer in God's time. God does not forget us. Our prayers are precious to God—like "tears in a bottle" they stand before God. They are in "a book of remembrance," which God keeps as a book of our prayers. We can be sure of God's attention—even as we wait for God to answer us.

REFLECTION QUESTION: In what ways do images such as "tears in a bottle" and "book of remembrance" help to establish faith in God's hearing and answering our prayers?

WORDS AND HEART

Matthew 6:5–8

W E all know people who seem to make a bit of a show about their religion. They seem to like to draw attention to themselves when they do "religious" things. We realize there is a great difference between these folks and those who genuinely try to live humble lives of obedience to God in Jesus Christ.

Jesus warned against those who carried out religious actions—such as prayer—without a true, heartfelt commitment and who made a show of their religion. Jesus called them "hypocrites" (Matt. 6:5). In Jesus's context, they "love to stand and pray in the synagogues and at the street corners, so that they may be seen by others." These folks drew attention—maybe even a crowd!—and turned their religion into a spectacle. Jesus warned that "they have received their reward." Attention from passersby is all they could expect. Their prayers were not genuine.

John Bunyan put it succinctly: "When thou prayest, rather let thy heart be without words, than thy words without a heart." Don't let your prayers be empty, hypocritical expressions—words without your heart in them. This is hypocritical.

It is far, far better to let your "heart be without words." Let the fullness of your heart be the reservoir from which your prayer is drawn. This is the true faith—springing from a heart fixed on God. God knows your heart. God will hear your prayer, however it is expressed.

PRAYER POINT: Try praying by realizing what is in your heart, focusing on it, and offering it to God, even without putting it into words.

BEGGING GOD'S BLESSINGS FOR ALL

Matthew 6:9

J ESUS'S model for prayer is the Lord's Prayer. It shows us what is essential for us to pray for . . . and to keep on praying for, every day.

The entrance to the Lord's Prayer is the address to God, "Our Father." This sets the tone for all that follows because Jesus taught that his disciples experience a parent-child relationship with God.

We often think of this in very individualistic terms. We have a personal relationship with God. But we should not substitute "Our Father" with "My Father." The prayer Jesus taught his disciples was for his whole body of disciples. When we pray this prayer, we are united with all other disciples of Jesus Christ, wherever they may be.

Ezekiel Hopkins caught this and wrote, "Since when we pray we must say, *Our Father*, this teaches us, to interest one another in our prayers. *Our Father* would not have us selfish so much as in our prayers, but in the very entrance into them, we are put in mind of the communion of saints, to beg those blessings, for all that belong to God which we ask for our selves. . . . When we go to God, we should bear upon our breasts the name of our brethren, and present them before God, through the intercession and mediation of Jesus Christ our Great High-Priest. . . . And this we ought to do both in public and private."

When we pray "Our Father," we beg blessings for all disciples of Jesus Christ.

PRAYER POINT: Pray the Lord's Prayer with a conscious sense of praying for and with the whole church. Pray specifically for your local congregation and those you know who are in need.

Amen!

Matthew 6:9–13

W E hear *Amen* in church. It ends all our prayers. Basically, the term means "so be it." I've heard it said that to put it in a contemporary idiom, *Amen* would mean "Yeah, that's what I say!"

We use the word to affirm or ratify what the prayer preceding it has said. It is the final word of approval to what has been prayed for and what we want God to hear. We conclude the Lord's Prayer this way. The last statements here are "For thine is the kingdom, and the power, and the glory, for ever." Then comes "Amen" (Matt. 6:13 KJV).

John Flavel commented on the word *Amen* at the end of the Lord's Prayer. He said it means that "all we pray for must be in a subserviency to God's kingdom, and with a desire of his glory." This prayer and every prayer should be focused on the two elements of God's "kingdom" and "glory." What else could be more important?

Our great desire should always be—whatever our prayers and whatever our actions—for God's glory and in service to God's reign or kingdom. As disciples of Jesus Christ, we are part of what God is doing in the world. All we do should witness to God's reign. All we do should be to bring glory to God's name. This is the big "umbrella" purpose of our lives. We cannot focus ourselves in any other direction or devote ourselves to anything less!

PRAYER POINT: Orient your prayers around the work of God's kingdom and all things that bring God glory. Ask God to enable you to be part of God's reign and a witness to God's glory.

O Lord my God and Heavenly Father . . .

Bless me at all times, both in hearing and reading thy Word. Give me the right use of all thy mercies, and corrections, that I may be the better for them. Let me abound in love to thy children. Let my heart be very nearly knit unto them, that where thou lovest most, there I may love most also. Let me watch and pray that I enter not into temptation: give me patience and contentment in all things. Let me love thee more and more, and the world less and less. So draw my mind upward, that I may despise all transitory things. Let me be so rapt and ravished with the sight and feeling of heavenly things, that I may make a base reckoning of all earthly things. Let me use this world, as though I used it not. Let me use it but for necessity, as meat and drink. Let me not be carried away with the vain pleasures and fond delights thereof. Good Father work the good work in me, and never leave me, nor forsake me, till thou has brought me to true happiness. Oh dear father, make me faithful in my calling, that I may serve thee in it, and be always careful to do what good I may in any thing.

Grant these petitions, most merciful God, not only to me, but to all thy dear children throughout the whole world, for Jesus Christ's sake. Amen.

ARTHUR DENT

GOD'S GOODNESS IN
TEACHING US TO PRAY

Matthew 6:9–13

SOMETIMES we take prayer for granted. We pray and then go on with our lives, not giving our prayers much more thought.

But being able to pray is a great gift! It is a gift God gives. In the Lord's Prayer, Jesus provided a prayer for his disciples that could become a pattern for their own prayers. This has been passed on to us through the Scriptures. Now we too can pray the prayer Jesus taught his disciples. Did you ever think what a great gift of grace this is and how blessed we are to be able to approach God in prayer? God is good!

William Gouge affirmed this when he wrote, "Behold, here the goodness of God, who is not only ready to hear us in his Son, but also by his Son hath taught us how to call upon him! Does he not herein show himself a Father indeed? Is not this a great motive to provoke us with boldness to go to the Throne of Grace? How much more effectually may we obtain what we ask in Christ's name, if we ask it in his form of prayer?"

Prayer is a gift of God's goodness. God hears us through Christ and teaches us how to call on God. We are bold to pray because God invites us to pray and gives us, as Gouge also said, "the perfect pattern of prayer" in the Lord's Prayer.

REFLECTION QUESTION: Think about the many ways in which prayer is key to your life. What would your life be like if gratitude for prayer was your main motivating factor for living?

Pray to Do God's Will

Matthew 6:10

"Your will be done" (Matt. 6:10). This petition from the Lord's Prayer may be one of the easiest, yet hardest, of the prayer's petitions. We could pray it casually: "Thy will be done"—"whatever will be, will be." But this is to abdicate our responsibility in seeking and doing God's will as a commitment of faith and love to God.

Or the petition may be hard for us. We relinquish our will to the will of God. We turn over our control of ourselves, our circumstances, and our futures to the will of God. This may be difficult.

To pray this petition, Ezekiel Hopkins wrote, "we need to pray, that God would incline our hearts to his Commandments, and then strengthen us to obey them: that as our will to good is the effect of his grace, so the effect of our wills may be the performances of his will."

We need to pray for God to help our attitudes to be those of obedience to what God wills, as expressed in the commandments of God, and to enable us to obey God's will as it comes to us. Then we can pray "Your will be done."

By God's grace, our wills are inclined toward desiring to do God's will. We should pray that with a will to do God's will, we may also receive God's grace so that we can carry out God's will. God's grace enables us to desire and to do God's will. Pray to do God's will!

Prayer Point: Pray through different areas of your life where you need to desire to do God's will. Then pray for God's grace to enable you to do God's will.

PRACTICE WHAT YOU PRAY

Matthew 6:12

W E are used to praying the Lord's Prayer and moving on to our other prayers. Or we may conclude our prayers with the Lord's Prayer and let the final *Amen* serve as a word for all our prayers. But what do we do after we have prayed the prayer? What are implications for our daily lives?

William Lyford suggested our duty when he wrote, "We must practice what we pray for: our actions must not cross our prayers. We must not pray and still rebel against God (Hosea 7.14). We must join our endeavors with our prayers."

We practice what we pray. When we pray "Forgive us our debts, as we also have forgiven our debtors" (Matt. 6:12), then we must forgive our debtors—those who have wronged us—if we expect to be forgiven by God. Our prayer for forgiveness finds its completion in our action of forgiving others.

When we pray "deliver us from evil," we should seek to stand against those evils which would attack us—personal and corporate and societal forms of evil. Our prayers for God's help against evils find completion in our facing up to the evils from which we hope to be delivered.

We cannot pray the Lord's Prayer as an automatic exercise— pray it and forget it. We must practice what we pray. We live out its implications daily, even as we entrust all things to the God who, in Jesus, invites us to pray and be heard!

REFLECTION QUESTION: Reflect on the implications of the Lord's Prayer for your daily life—in what you think and what you do. Can you make improvements?

In the Day of Temptation

Matthew 6:13

T EMPTATIONS afflict us all. We cannot avoid them, but we do not have to give in to them. Our hope is that we can withstand temptations, turning away from them and not letting ourselves be drawn into their net. An adage often attributed to Martin Luther says that we cannot prevent birds from flying over our heads, but we can prevent them from making a nest in our hair!

To resist temptations to sin, we need God's help. We are not strong enough to resist the tempter's power on our own. Because we need God's power, we pray in the Lord's Prayer "Lead us not into temptation" (Matt. 6:13 RSV).

We pray to resist temptation to sin in all dimensions of life, as well as temptation to sin in ways toward which we are particularly weak and vulnerable. These are "general sins" and "specific sins." As Thomas Gouge wrote, "Often have recourse unto God by fervent prayer, as against sin in general, that he would be pleased to keep thee from falling thereunto, so especially against those particular sins which you find working and stirring in yourself, and with which you are most molested, earnestly begging power and strength from God, that you may be enabled to stand in the day of temptation."

We pray to stand in the day of temptation—a day that comes to us every day! God's help is our only hope. Pray "Lead us not into temptation."

PRAYER POINT: Pray fervently for God's help in resisting temptations—the temptations that always surround you and the specific temptations to which you are susceptible.

WHY GOD DESIRES OUR PRAYERS

Matthew 7:7–11

D o you ever wonder why God desires our prayers? If God desires to bless us or give us good gifts, God could do that without our asking God for gifts and blessing in prayers of petition and supplication. Why does God want us to pray?

Jesus told his disciples that they are to ask, search, and knock in prayer, for "everyone who asks receives, and everyone who searches finds, and for everyone who knocks, the door will be opened" (Matt. 7:8). He went on to say that if a parent will give good gifts to their child, "how much more will your Father in heaven give good things to those who ask him!" (v. 11).

When we ask, search, and knock in prayer and receive God's answers and "good things," we know the origin and source of our blessings is God. Anthony Burgess wrote that "God will be sought to because hereby he is acknowledged the author and fountain of all the good we have." Prayer shows us God is the source of all the good we receive. Through faith, we see the gifts of God—gifts for which we may have prayed from God! Burgess continued that whoever "lives without prayer lives as if there were no God as if all things came by a natural necessity or uncertain chance, and not from a wise God."

Let us pray and thank God!

PRAYER POINT: Devote your prayer to praising and thanking God—for all the gifts and blessings you have received and, most of all, for God's desire that we pray to God.

Praying and Living

Matthew 23:1–12

THERE is a danger we all face. It is the potential disconnect between what we say we believe and how we live. This is the yawning chasm between promise and performance. It is the contradiction between what we say and what we do.

Jesus spotted this in the lives of contemporaries, of whom he said, "They do not practice what they teach" (Matt. 23:3). This is a negative example of what Jesus wanted—and expected—from his own disciples. Jesus's words stand as a warning to us to live consistently so that what we believe will be expressed in how we live. As John Owen put it, "He who prays as he ought, will endeavor to live as he prays. This none can do who doth not with diligence keep his heart unto the things he hath prayed about. To pray *earnestly* and live *carelessly*, is to proclaim a man is not Spiritually minded in his prayer."

Praying and living must be congruent. We must live as we pray. What we pray for should express what we live for as Jesus's disciples who seek to be obedient to the will of God. We must always be on watch for ways in which our "talk" and our "walk" do not go together, under God. If others point this out to us, we should take heed. We must not "pray earnestly and live carelessly" lest we too fall under Jesus's condemnation.

PRAYER POINT: Ask God to point out ways in which your life is not a faithful witness to what you believe in your Christian faith. Repent and live as God desires.

O MOST mighty and eternal God, who art the Creator, Guider, Governor and Preserver of all things, both in heaven and earth; vouchsafe, we humbly beseech thee, to look down with the eye of pity and compassion upon us miserable and wretched sinners; who at this time are prostrate here before thee, to offer up this our sacrifice of prayer and thanksgiving unto thee. . . .

O merciful Lord, and loving Father, remember the infirmities of thy frail servants, assisting our weak souls with thy grace, that in all things we may love, honor, and obey thy heavenly will and majesty, waking and walking in the paths of righteousness to the scope of perfect holiness, condemning this witching world, with all her foolish illusions, for the true glorifying of thy name, through Jesus Christ our Lord, Amen.

WILLIAM PERKINS

A Gracious Calm in the Soul

Mark 4:35–41

T HE story of Jesus calming the storm is a wonderful example of Jesus's power, love, and way of bringing peace in the midst of the most dangerous situations. At Jesus's word, "the wind ceased, and there was a dead calm" (Mark 4:39). By extension, this shows Christ's presence with us in life and his power to calm the storms in our lives, even when all seems to be chaos and we are afraid.

Thomas Watson alluded to this story in relation to prayer. He wrote, "Prayer does to the heart, as Christ did to the sea, when it was tempestuous, he rebuked the wind, and there was a great calm; so when the passions are up, and the will is apt to mutiny against God, Prayer makes a gracious calm in the soul: Prayer does to the heart as the Sponge to the Cannon, when hot cools it."

We all need calm in the soul in the midst of the storms we face, whatever they are. We cannot provide this calm ourselves. Our help needs to come from beyond ourselves—from Jesus Christ. We know what it is like to have our passions stirred up and our will "apt to mutiny against God." We need our passions stilled and our will open to God's will, trusting our Savior to bring peace and calm.

Will we turn over our stormy temperaments to Jesus in prayer? Or will we continue to churn and be agitated? Hear Jesus say, "Peace! Be still!" (v. 39).

PRAYER POINT: Take all the disturbing situations in your life and turn them over to Jesus in prayer. Hear Jesus's word of peace as you pray.

LOVE TO NEIGHBOR AND LOVE TO GOD

Mark 12:28–34

WHEN it comes to the basics Jesus wants from his disciples, his twofold summary of the Law of God is primary. Jesus was asked "Which commandment is the first of all?" (Mark 12:28). He replied, "The first is, 'Hear, O Israel: the Lord our God, the Lord is one; you shall love the Lord your God with all your heart, and with all your soul, and with all your mind, and with all your strength.' The second is this, 'You shall love your neighbor as yourself'" (vv. 29–31). Love God, and love your neighbor.

Nathaniel Vincent explored some implications of Jesus's response in relation to prayer. He wrote, "Love is to be acted in prayer. There must be a love to our neighbor, and they must from the heart be forgiven, that have trespassed against us; shall we think much of a few pence, when we are debtors [of] many thousand talents? But principally, there must be love to the Lord expressed in prayer, his favor and fellowship with him must be longed for."

"Love is to be acted in prayer"—and very practically in loving our neighbor. This love is expressed in forgiveness from the heart when we have been wronged. This is not easy. But if we pray, we love—and we forgive.

To be honest, we know that what is "owed" us is infinitesimally small compared to what we owe God. A sense of proportionality helps here. "Love to the Lord" is the primary love expressed in prayer. Love your neighbor; love God.

PRAYER POINT: Pray to love and forgive your neighbor and to love and be forgiven by God. Keep these two focuses in front of you, and long for God's favor and fellowship.

By Prayer We Learn to Pray

Luke 11:1

"Lord, teach us to pray" (Luke 11:1). This was the request of one of Jesus's disciples. Jesus answered the request by giving his disciples—and us—the "Lord's Prayer," a model for all our prayers and the enduring prayer we offer to God.

We learn by doing. We've heard that expression. We like our airplane pilots to have had the practical experience of actually flying a plane before we entrust ourselves to their care!

So, too, with prayer. By praying, we learn to pray. Richard Sibbes put it this way: "As every grace increases by exercise of itself, so doth the grace of prayer; by prayer we learn to pray."

The more we practice or live the graces God has given, the stronger they become—like exercise of the body. So we pray. We learn and continue to learn the depths of prayer as we pray. This should encourage us! The more we pray, the deeper our experience of prayer can become. Our faith becomes stronger, and the grace of God will become more real and meaningful to us.

Some think prayer is just theoretical—words we utter. But it is really the most practical thing in the world. In prayer—in the tradition of the Lord's Prayer—we address God, express our needs, and praise God's reign and glory. What could be more intensely "real world" than the reality of God—who God is and what God does—in this world? Let us learn to pray . . . by praying!

REFLECTION QUESTIONS: In what ways have you grown in grace through your life of prayer? Do you receive new insights about prayer through your practice of praying?

HALLOWED BE THY NAME

Luke 11:2

W HEN we pray the Lord's Prayer, we say "Hallowed be your name" (Luke 11:2), and we may wonder what this means. We don't use the word *hallow* much—except as part of *Halloween*!

The word *hallow* means "to make holy." This is what we pray in the Lord's Prayer: may God's name be made holy throughout the earth.

In his catechism, Richard Greenham asked, "How shall God's name be declared to be holy and glorious?" He answered, "First, we pray that his wisdom, power, goodness, mercy, truth, righteousness, and eternity, may more and more be imparted and manifested unto us and other of God's people. Secondly, we pray, that according as we know these things, so the fruits of them may appear in our, and other [of] God's peoples' lives, that so God's name may be honored and praised."

It may be quite a while since we listed—even in our minds—all the attributes of God that Greenham mentions as aspects of "hallowing" God's name! But these are all dimensions of the Lord, and at least some of them may come to mind when we utter this phrase.

Then, practically, may we experience the "fruits" of who God is in our lives and in the lives of others so that "God's name may be honored and praised." All dimensions of who God is should be praised and honored in our lives. "Hallowed be thy name"!

PRAYER POINT: Pray a prayer hallowing God's name by thinking of all these attributes or aspects of God. Pray that the meanings of these aspects may be expressed and lived out in your life.

PRAY FOR THE SPIRIT

Luke 11:5–13

THERE are times when it is difficult to pray. We may pray without sensing God's presence or power. Prayer may seem routine, lacking strong direction or energy.

In these times, we should pray for the Spirit. The Holy Spirit calls us to pray, enables our prayers, and directs us in our prayers to God. So when our prayer life is weak, we need to pray for God's Spirit to be with us and help. Jesus said God gives the gift of the Holy Spirit "to those who ask him" (Luke 11:13). And God helps us to pray for the Spirit.

Henry Scudder put it this way: "Pray for the Spirit; and though you cannot pray well without the Spirit, yet since it is God's will that you should pray for [the Spirit], set about prayer for [the Spirit] as well as you can; then God will enable you to pray for the Spirit, and you shall have [the Spirit]. For Christ saith, 'If ye that are evil know how to give good gifts to your children, how much more shall your heavenly Father give the Holy Spirit to them that ask him?' As these are means to get the Spirit, so they are means to continue, nourish, and increase the graces of the Spirit."

God's Spirit enables our prayer, continuing to nurture and nourish the graces we receive by the Spirit—this is, the "fruit of the Spirit," love, joy, peace, and more (Gal. 5:22). Pray for the Spirit!

PRAYER POINT: Make it a point to pray for God's Spirit before you pray and as you pray. Trust the Spirit to lead and guide your prayers and to be active in your life of discipleship.

Praying for the Wicked

Luke 23:32–38

J esus's crucifixion was marked by his agonizing death between two criminals. Here was the gross injustice of putting to death the innocent, sinless Son of God. If ever anyone had motives for revenge or payback, it was Jesus.

Instead, astonishingly, we hear Jesus say from the cross, "Father, forgive them; for they do not know what they are doing" (Luke 23:34). At the edge of death, Jesus spoke forgiveness, asking God to forgive those who were wicked beyond words.

In his death, Jesus embodied the teachings of his life—loving and forgiving others, no matter how much or how deeply they have hurt and wronged us (see Luke 6:37).

We are to forgive others who have hurt and wronged us. We are also to pray for them, asking God to forgive them, as Jesus did on the cross. Anthony Burgess wrote that "it is our duty to pray for the wicked though wallowing in their sins, that they may be converted and brought home to God." This is an ongoing call to prayer for others whose attitudes and actions are against God's will and purposes and whose lives are marked by sins that express hearts in opposition to God or total disregard for God.

We pray for friends and loved ones. Do we pray for those who do evil, that God's Spirit may lead them to faith in Jesus Christ the Savior?

PRAYER POINT: Today, pray for those who do not know Jesus Christ as Savior, remembering especially those whose actions and deeds mark them in the eyes of others as especially sinful.

LORD, let not the darkness of ignorance comprehend us.

Lead us by the continual light of thy grace to work righteousness.

Let us not sleep in sin, O God.

Quicken our weak souls against earthly sluggishness.

Give us the heavenly rest of thy unspeakable peace, O Lord:

And nourish us with thy grace to salvation.

Lord, comfort the needy, the sick, the prisoned, the tormented, the distressed, and helpless, with the presence of thy grace: and have mercy upon them, and us.

Pitifully hear our complaints, O dear Father, and grant our requests, for thy sweet Son's sake, our Savior. Amen.

WILLIAM PERKINS

Lifting the Heart to God

John 14:13–17

W E make our prayers to God the Father, or Jesus Christ the Son, or God the Holy Spirit. We may usually "default" to God the Father, but we know the whole Trinity is involved in our prayers. So it is appropriate to direct our prayers to Father, Son, or Holy Spirit. As we do, however, we know the persons of the Godhead act together, each carrying out divine action. In prayer, the three persons of the Trinity all participate.

Edward Leigh wrote, "Prayer is a lifting up of the heart to God our Father in the name and mediation of Christ through the Spirit, whereby we desire the good things he hath promised in his Word, and according to his will."

The whole Trinity is active in our prayers in which we lift up our hearts to the Lord. Jesus Christ is the mediator between God and humanity and represents us before God the Father (see Rom. 8:34). The Holy Spirit abides in us and enables our prayers (see John 14:17; Gal. 5:5). As we lift our hearts to God, we express a desire for the "good things" Scripture promises us, and we ask that these things be in accord with God's will.

This is our great confidence in prayer. When we pray, we have God's "full attention"—Father, Son, and Holy Spirit. All work together in providing for our prayers, answering our prayers, and leading us into further prayer and obedience to God. Lift your heart to the Lord in prayer!

REFLECTION QUESTION: Think of your prayers and recall to which member of the Godhead they are usually addressed. In what ways would your prayers be different—or the same—if you addressed another member of the Godhead?

THE HAND OF THE SOUL

Acts 17:22–28

WHEN Paul was in Athens, he debated in the Areopagus with philosophers. He told them their city was full of objects of worship, including an altar with the inscription "To an unknown god" (Acts 17:23). But Paul proclaimed this "unknown god" was really the "God who made the world and everything in it, he who is Lord of heaven and earth" (v. 24). Then he quoted a Greek poet who wrote "in him we live and move and have our being" (v. 28). The "unknown god" is really the God who is known as the Savior Paul proclaimed, Jesus Christ.

In God we "have our being" and all else that enables our lives to be sustained. One of these essentials for life is prayer. John Downame wrote that "seeing our wants are continual, and God hath appointed prayer as the hand of the soul, to be thrust into his rich Treasury of all grace and goodness for a continual supply, without which we can have no assurance, that we shall receive any thing at the hands of God; hereby it manifestly appears that our prayers also ought to be daily and continual."

Prayer is "the hand of the soul" by which we receive God's grace and goodness. Since we "live and move and have our being in God," our "wants are continual." God graciously permits our prayers to be ways by which we receive all we need from God's own hand. Pray to God!

> **PRAYER POINT:** As you pray, think of receiving God's grace and goodness through the outstretched hand of your prayer. In this way, we perceive God's blessings as directly given to us.

INFINITE and Eternal Majesty, Author and Fountain of Being and Blessedness, how little do we poor sinful creatures know of Thee, or the way to serve and please Thee? . . .

Blessed be thine infinite mercy who sent thine own Son to dwell among men, and instruct them by his example as well as his laws, giving them a perfect pattern of what they ought to be. O that the holy life of the blessed Jesus may be always in my thoughts, and before mine eyes, till I receive a deep sense and impression of those excellent graces that shined so eminently in him, and let me never remit my endeavors till that new and divine nature prevail in my soul, and Christ be formed within me. Amen.

HENRY SCOUGAL

PRAY WITH CONFIDENCE

Romans 4:16–25

PEOPLE ask us to believe they will do what they promise. We get barraged in TV commercials and other places by people making promises about products that are supposed to do wonderful things. We are asked to believe what the spokespersons say and what they promise.

But we've all had less than success with products we buy; many do not perform as advertised or deliver what was promised.

How different is God! William Gouge wrote, "That we pray with confidence in God's almighty power: believing that God is able to grant whatsoever we shall ask according to his will. As the title 'Father' gave us ground of confidence in God's fatherly love: so this placing of him in heaven, giveth us as good ground of confidence in his power. Thus shall we (as Abraham did) give glory to God, being fully persuaded that what he hath promised he is able also to perform."

To believe God will fulfill what God promises gives us confidence for our prayers. The God who is our "Father" is the God of Abraham and Sarah, who fulfilled the promise to them that they would have an offspring even at very advanced ages. Abraham did not waver with distrust, but "he gave glory to God, being fully convinced that God was able to do what he had promised" (Rom. 4:20–21).

God will do what God has promised to us! We can pray with confidence!

REFLECTION QUESTION: What helps you to maintain your confidence in prayer? What difference does it make whether or not you pray with confidence?

CHRIST'S PRAYERS BRING ACCEPTANCE OF OURS

Romans 8:31–39

W E often conclude our prayers by saying "In Jesus's name" or "in the name of Jesus Christ our Lord." We are invoking Jesus Christ to hear our prayers and are seeking the power and help of Jesus Christ in bringing our prayers forth.

Paul speaks of Jesus's ministry of intercession—of presenting our prayers to God. He wrote, "It is Christ Jesus, who died, yes, who was raised, who is at the right hand of God, who indeed intercedes for us" (Rom. 8:34). The book of Hebrews also says, "He is able for all time to save those who approach God through him, since he always lives to make intercession for them" (Heb. 7:25).

A model here is Jesus's great high priestly prayer for his disciples in John 17. Anthony Burgess wrote that "this prayer of Christ sanctifies all our prayers. They become accepted of God through him. . . . As our tears need washing in his blood, so our prayers need Christ's prayer. He prayed that our prayers may be received. . . . Though I am unworthy yet Christ is worthy to be heard."

We can have no greater assurance when we pray than realizing our prayers are being received by God through the mediation and intercession of our Lord Jesus Christ, the perfect sacrifice for our sins (see Heb. 7:27; 10:12). God accepts our prayers through Jesus Christ our Lord. We depend on Christ for our prayers to be heard. What joy and comfort!

PRAYER POINT: Make a point to think of how Jesus actively intercedes for you when you pray. This reminds us that we never pray alone but instead always pray through the work of Jesus Christ on our behalf.

The Voice and Flame of Faith

Romans 10:1–4

T IME and again, we need to remember that prayers are an expression of faith. Faith in God, in Jesus Christ, is conveyed to us by the power of the Holy Spirit by our prayers. Prayer is rooted in faith as the expression of our confidence that God hears and answers prayer. Prayer is not a scientific exercise to prove God's power to answer or determine God's goodwill toward us. We pray from the stirrings of the Spirit within us— our "heart's desire and prayer" (Rom. 10:1). We express our love and trust in God, our Creator, and our Redeemer Jesus Christ. We pray from faith, in faith.

Richard Sibbes put it this way: "For prayer is nothing but the voice of faith, the flame of faith, the fire is in the heart and spirit, but the voice, the flame, the expression of faith is prayer, faith in the heart sets prayer to work."

Faith emerges from the fire in our hearts and the Spirit of God within us. Our voice in prayer expresses that which is deep in our hearts. When faith is in our hearts, our prayers will burst into flame!

God works in relation to our prayers, carrying out divine purposes and answering our prayers according to God's will and providence for our lives. The voice and flame of our faith is our prayer!

REFLECTION QUESTION: In what ways are you conscious of your prayers being prompted by the Holy Spirit as conscious expressions of your faith?

For the Spirit of Illumination

Romans 15:1–6

THE Holy Scriptures are central to the life of the church and to our own lives as individuals. The Bible is the Word of God, God's loving and gracious gift to show us what to believe and how to live.

The Scriptures meet us in all of life, communicating God's Word and God's will. We need to listen to Scripture and interpret it so "by steadfastness and by the encouragement of the scripture we might have hope" (Rom. 15:4).

Often in worship services, before the Scriptures are read and the sermon is preached, there is a "prayer for illumination." The Spirit of God is invoked to bless the reading and understanding of God's Word as it comes to us. A basic Protestant theological conviction is that God's Word and God's Spirit are inextricably bound together.

We should also pray for the Spirit of illumination as we read and listen to Scripture in our own lives. Thomas Gouge urged, "Lift up thine heart in prayer unto God [prior to reading Scripture], as for the Spirit of Illumination, to open the eyes of thine understanding, that thou may rightly conceive his Word: so for wisdom to apply, memory to retain, faith to believe, and grace to practice what thou shalt read."

Gouge gives us important guidance on what to ask of the Spirit: wisdom, memory, faith, and grace—for the purposes God desires Scripture to carry out in our lives. Pray for the Spirit of illumination!

> **PRAYER POINT:** Before reading the Bible, get in the habit of asking God's Spirit to illumine your heart and mind as you read Scripture, to help you interpret it, and to help you to live out its message in your life.

BENEFITS OF ONE ANOTHER'S PRAYERS

1 Corinthians 12:14–26

P AUL'S description of the Christian church in 1 Corinthians 12:14–26 is pretty clear. The church is one and has many members. All members are one with each other and with Christ. All were baptized into one body. Put succinctly, "there are many members, yet one body" (v. 20).

Paul goes on to speak of the relationships those in the body of Christ are to have with each other: Members are to "care for one another" (v. 25). For "if one member suffers, all suffer together with it" (v. 26).

One expression of care we can make for the whole church is to pray for the church and all its members. William Gouge wrote, "When we pray, we pray not for one, but for the whole Church, because we are all one. . . . A great comfort it must needs be to such weak ones, as cannot pray as they desire. The privilege of the communion of saints, in nothing more appears, than in the mutual participation of one another's prayers."

We are one with each other in the communion of saints. This means we mutually participate in one another's lives and we pray for one another—the whole body of Christ—to express this care and love that Jesus directly commanded when he said, "Love one another" (John 13:34).

In the church, we receive the benefits of each other's prayers. Thank God! We should bless others by praying daily for the whole body of the church.

> **REFLECTION QUESTIONS:** How faithful are you in praying for the whole church? Do you pray frequently? Do you think that imagining the church as a fellowship of love would stimulate you to pray for the church more often?

THE POWER AND PROMISE OF GOD

2 Corinthians 1:15–22

W E conclude the Lord's Prayer with the familiar words "For thine is the kingdom, and the power, and the glory, for ever. Amen" (Matt. 6:13 KJV). These words gather up the whole prayer that has preceded. All we have prayed for in praising God's name and in the petitions of the prayer are now drawn together in the great vision of God's powerful and glorious kingdom. The God whose kingdom will come (see v. 10) will triumph in power and glory to bring the kingdom that is "for ever"!

Robert Hill suggested two uses for this conclusion to the Lord's Prayer: "That in our prayers we ever debase our selves, and ascribe all glory to this King of Kings. . . . In our prayers to be ever persuaded of the power of God, that he can help us, and the promise of God that he will help us." He refers to Paul's teaching that in Jesus Christ "every one of God's promises is a 'Yes.' For this reason it is through him that we say the 'Amen,' to the glory of God" (2 Cor. 1:20).

In Jesus, all God's promises come to pass, as will God's kingdom. God's reign will not be thwarted by anything in all creation, including forces of evil. All hope and glory go to God's coming kingdom. Here and now God can help us—and promises to help us. Take hope in all situations. The power and promise of God are sure and certain!

PRAYER POINT: Conclude your prayers with an affirmation of God's help and promise to help in the coming of God's kingdom. Put trust in that promise, and let it bring you hope.

LORD . . .

Oh that thou wouldst become a God in covenant with us, and a reconciled Father to us, and let us be the sons and daughters of the Lord Almighty. Let us be no more strangers and foreigners, but fellow-citizens with the saints, and of the household of God.

Send forth the spirit of thy Son into our hearts, crying, Abba Father. Deliver us from fear and bondage, and seal us up unto the day of redemption. Say unto us, souls I am your salvation. . . . Let thy spirit bear witness with our spirits, that we are the children, and not only children, but heirs, heirs of God, joint-heirs with Christ unto the inheritance that is undefiled, and will never fade away, reserved in heaven for us. . . .

O Lord . . .

Let our conversations be as becomes the Gospel; help us to follow thee as dear children, to live as the redeemed of the Lord, and to glorify thee in our bodies and in our spirits: For we are not our own, but are bought with a price. We profess Christ; let us depart from iniquity, and walk even as he walked. Not contenting ourselves with the forms of Godliness without the power of Godliness.

Let us not profess to know thee, and in works deny thee; but make us zealous of good works, considering we are created unto good works, which God has before ordained, that we should walk in them. Help us to do justly, and to love mercy, and to walk humbly with God. Amen.

NATHANIEL VINCENT

WAIT ON GOD'S TIME

Galatians 4:1–7

IN prayer there is one lesson we need to learn over and over again: we must wait on God's time. It is a hard lesson to learn and follow, but we know it is true.

God hears and answers our prayers, but God's answers come in God's time rather than our own. This is "the fullness of time." The people of Israel waited long for a Messiah. But as Paul wrote, "when the fullness of time had come, God sent his Son, born of a woman, born under the law" (Gal. 4:4). God sent Jesus Christ to redeem us at the time God chose.

William Perkins commented on this verse in Galatians with wise advice: "This must teach us, when by prayer we ask any good thing at God's hand, not to prescribe any time unto God, but to leave it to his providence. Again, if thou live in any misery, wait on the Lord, and be content. For that is the fit and best time of thy deliverance, which God hath appointed."

We trust God's timing—God's providence—for the best time for answers to our prayers. If God chose the best timing for sending Jesus, how much more will God choose the best timing to answer our prayers. In the midst of our waiting—even our "misery"—we trust God and remain content.

It is hard to wait. But we wait for the "fit and best time" of our deliverance and God's answers. We wait . . . and trust God's time!

REFLECTION QUESTION: Think about the times you had to wait—and wait long—for God's answers to your prayers. What can you do to keep focused on waiting for God's time?

TALK LESS AND PRAY MORE

Galatians 5:22–26

W E may think we can solve our problems. We face something, think about it, talk about it, and act. We don't see the need for prayer.

But we cannot handle everything ourselves. In the world around us, can we by talk alone or our efforts alone meet all needs?

We know we cannot. God invites our prayers so that we can unburden ourselves of thinking we can do it all or solve all problems. Instead of living by our own strength, we should "live by the Spirit" and "be guided by the Spirit" (Gal. 5:25). Trust God. The Spirit of God who comes to us in prayer can lead us and guide us in God's best ways.

John Owen wrote that "if we would talk less, and pray more about them, things would be better than they are in the world; at least we should be better enabled to bear them and undergo our portion in them with the more satisfaction."

We need to turn all things over to God. The fruit of God's Spirit will give us what we need to face all things—"love, joy, peace, patience, kindness . . ." (v. 22). Not talk, but prayer is what we need. God's Spirit can work in and through us in prayer and for action. The Spirit enables us to face our needs and help with the needs of others. Ask God's Spirit to lead you. Talk less, and pray more!

REFLECTION QUESTION: Think of times when you have tried to do everything by yourself. What brought you to realize that you needed to pray and ask for God's Spirit to help you?

MAKING REQUESTS AND OFFERING THANKS

Ephesians 6:18–20

THE Puritans agreed with John Calvin and other Protestant Reformers that prayer was the chief "exercise" or "expression" of faith. The clearest thing we can do to show our faith is to pray to God. Prayer is the rhythm of our Christian lives. It is our breath, our heartbeat. We take seriously the image given in Ephesians: "Pray in the Spirit at all times in every prayer and supplication" (Eph. 6:18).

In prayer we call on God, we talk with God, we listen to God. Our prayers take many forms and occur in many times. Through them all, the focus is on God, especially who God is and what God has done—supremely in Jesus Christ our Lord.

The two main parts of prayer are thanksgiving and petition. We thank God for all things, and we pray to God about all things. We express our thanksgiving and our desires as we share what is in our hearts with our Lord. Paul Baynes put it well when he wrote that "prayer is an opening of the heart to God, in making requests, and offering thanks through Christ. For the nature of it is nothing but a motion of the soul in desire and thanksgiving; called the lifting up of, or the rearing up of, the soul." As the psalmist cried, "To you, O LORD, I lift up my soul" (Ps. 25:1).

Do we pray "at all times"? Do we thank God? Do we make requests of God? Keep focused on lifting up your soul in prayer!

PRAYER POINT: In your prayer, find what is in your heart—the thanksgiving you can offer to God and the requests you want to make to God. Conclude by praising God.

CASTING OUR CARE ON THE LORD

Philippians 4:4–7

CARES confront us. Life brings many cares to us. We face situations or things or people that bring us anxieties and worries. We cannot shake these burdens alone. It's been said that worry is like a rocking chair—you go back and forth and never get anywhere!

This is why we need Paul's advice. He wrote, "Do not worry about anything, but in everything by prayer and supplication with thanksgiving let your requests be made known to God" (Phil. 4:6). The antidote for worry is prayer. As we pray in thanksgiving and ask God for help, we will find "the peace of God, which surpasses all understanding, will guard your hearts and your minds in Christ Jesus" (v. 7). Thomas Taylor summarized this succinctly: "In nothing be carefull, but let your requests be shown. . . . Prayer is a casting of our care on the Lord: therefore call upon on him, and commend your wants unto him."

Worries and cares can be met by the power of prayer. To cast our care on the Lord in prayer can relieve our worries. Worries may persist. But they will be put into perspective when we realize God is there and will see us through. Paul's words remind us of the words to the psalmist: "Cast your burden on the LORD, and he will sustain you" (Ps. 55:22).

We are sustained by the peace of God. God's peace is beyond our understanding. But it keeps our hearts and minds in Christ Jesus.

PRAYER POINT: Name your deepest worries and anxieties and then express them before God. Ask God for peace to sustain you physically and emotionally and keep you secure in Jesus Christ.

EFFECTS OF OUR PRAYERS

1 Thessalonians 3:6–10

I T is gratifying to have your prayers answered. To know that God has heard and granted your request is a cause for great gratitude and thanksgiving.

But there is also a tremendous sense of thanksgiving when you have joined your prayers for another person or people with the prayers of others and have seen those prayers answered by God.

Paul was heartened by Timothy's report about the faith and love of the Christians he had just visited in Thessalonica. Paul wrote to the Thessalonians, "How can we thank God enough for you in return for all the joy that we feel before our God because of you?" (1 Thess. 3:9). He said, "Night and day we pray most earnestly" (v. 10). Paul and others were praying for the Thessalonian Christians and, according to Timothy, the church there was growing in faith and love.

Thomas Goodwin captured this joy in joint prayer for others when he wrote, "If God give you a heart thankful for a blessing vouchsafed [granted] to another, prayed for by you with others, it is another sign your prayers have had some hand in it." There is profound gratitude and thanksgiving when our prayers are joined with others in the church and we see the effects of answered prayer. The "communion of saints" binds us together in Christ's church, and we "pray for one another" (James 5:16)!

REFLECTION QUESTION: Think of times when you have joined with believers in the church to pray for other people or situations. What feelings did you have when those prayers were answered?

102

PRAYER AND THANKS

1 Thessalonians 3:9-10

PAUL was a person of prayer. He constantly prayed for others—both for individuals and for churches. Paul knew that all things happen through God's will and by God's grace. So he prayed for others whom he loved and for the churches that were growing in God's grace and faithful discipleship in Jesus Christ.

Paul told the Thessalonians, "How can we thank God enough for you in return for all the joy that we feel before our God because of you?" (1 Thess. 3:9). Paul's prayers were always with the church (see v. 10), and what God was doing among the Thessalonians was a cause for deep joy.

Prayer and *thanks*. These two words described Paul's life. They mark our lives too. We are thankful for sins forgiven and for mercies and blessings given to us by God. We pray in thankfulness and petition, fully thankful when our prayers are answered.

Thomas Goodwin said, "Prayer and thanks are like the double motion of the lungs, the air that is sucked in by prayer, is breathed forth again by thanks." This is a good image for us. Breathe in by prayer; breathe out in thanks. What better rhythm for life in Christ could we imagine? As breathing is necessary for physical life to continue, so prayer and thanks are necessary for our spiritual life—at every moment!

Do we consciously pray and thank God—as regularly as breathing? Let us commit ourselves to recognizing this vital role of praying and thanking.

REFLECTION QUESTION: What difference does it make in Christian living when we keep the images of prayer and thanks before us as the rhythm of our life in Christ?

Good God!

What a mighty felicity is this to which we are called? How graciously hast thou joined our duty and happiness together, and prescribed that for our work, the performance whereof is a great reward?

O the happiness of those souls that have broken the fetters of self-love, and disentangled their affection from every narrow and particular good, whose understandings are enlightened by thy Holy Spirit, and their wills enlarged to the extent of thine, who love thee above all things, and all mankind for thy sake! . . .

 O teach me to do thy will, for thou art my God, thy Spirit is good, lead me unto the land of uprightness. Quicken me, O Lord, for thy Name's sake, and perfect that which concerns me: Thy mercy, O Lord, endures for ever, forsake not the works of thine own hands. Amen.

HENRY SCOUGAL

PRAY CONTINUALLY

1 Thessalonians 5:16–18

BEING a Christian is a full-time vocation! We are to be Christians 24-7, giving our whole selves to God in Jesus Christ, as Christ's disciples.

To do this, we need constant contact with our Lord. We need prayer—conversation between us and God. This prayer contact gives us life, keeping our relationship with God in Christ vital and alive.

No wonder Paul urged the Thessalonians to "pray without ceasing" (1 Thess. 5:17). We cannot live as well without praying; we neglect prayer at our own risk. Instead, we pray to express our constant thanks and gratitude to God—continually.

Our prayers do not need to be vocal to be heard by God and to keep our conversation with God alive. William Perkins wrote, "Pray continually, I mean not by solemn and set prayer, but by secret and inward [utterances] of the heart, that is, by a continual elevation of mind unto Christ, sitting at the right hand of God the Father, and that either by prayer, or giving of thanks, so often as any occasion shall be offered."

We should always have our God in our minds. As Perkins suggests, our minds need to be elevated to think of Jesus Christ, who is seated at the right hand of God the Father. The risen, exalted Christ is before us, calling us into praise and thanks through all the moments of our lives!

REFLECTION QUESTIONS: What techniques can help you pray "without ceasing" or "continually"? Are these helps you will put into practice in your life?

PRAYER SWEETENS THE MERCY

1 Thessalonians 5:16–18

THE saints of God have always been people of prayer. Prayer is our lifeline with God. Without prayer, our lives lose their way. Prayer should be a practice in which we always engage. We want to follow Paul's prescription: "Pray without ceasing" (1 Thess. 5:17).

Just as prayer is our conversation with God, what we receive in prayer, we can return to God in gratitude. Thomas Manton recognized this when he wrote, "They that pray often see all things come from God, and they return all to God again; they take it out of his hands, and use it for his glory. Usually what we win by prayer we wear with thanksgiving. Others do not and cannot observe providence as much as they do that pray often and upon all occasions look to God. Besides, prayer sweetens the mercy."

We return blessings we have been given by God through prayer—for God's glory. Manton mentioned Hannah, who prayed in the temple for a son. God answered her, and she said, "For this child I prayed; and the LORD has granted me the petition that I made to him. Therefore I have lent him to the LORD; as long as he lives, he is given to the LORD" (1 Sam. 1:27–28). She dedicated Samuel to the Lord, who used him as a prophet. We pray continually and receive God's good gifts. Then we return them to the Lord. Prayer sweetens the mercy!

REFLECTION QUESTIONS: Think of God's answers to your prayers. In what ways have you been able to return the blessing and all things back to God? Did prayer make the mercy you received sweeter?

Pray for Others

2 Thessalonians 1:5–12

W E are always tempted to make our prayers self-centered. We ask God, again and again, for what we want, what we think is best, and what we need. God does want to hear our needs. But there is more to prayer.

The "more" is that we also need an "outward focus" to our prayers. We need to pray for the world, the church, and for others. Our prayers lift up needs beyond our own.

Thomas Watson gave illustrations of this from nature when he wrote, "Let us pray for others as well as for our selves. . . . Spiders work only for themselves, but bees work for the good of others. . . . The springs refresh others with their crystal streams; the sun enlightens others with its golden beams; the more a Christian is ennobled with grace, the more he besieges heaven with his prayers for others. If we are members of the Body mystical, we cannot but have a sympathy with others in their wants, and this sympathy sets us a praying for them."

God's grace in our lives leads us to "besiege heaven" on behalf of others. Do we pray with this kind of passion for those in need? Our hearts reach out in care for others, so our hearts should also reach out in prayer for others.

Paul serves as our model. He wrote to the Thessalonians, "We always pray for you" (2 Thess. 1:11). Our prayers are the arms of love reaching to embrace those whose lives need to be blessed.

Prayer Point: Devote your prayer to the needs of others: those throughout the world, those in the church, and those of your own acquaintance. Ask God to bless those people and entrust them to God's care.

Pray for the Saints of All Nations

1 Timothy 2:1–7

THE church of Jesus Christ extends throughout the world. We are united by faith with sisters and brothers in Christ all over the globe. This is one aspect of the "communion of saints," which we confess in the Apostles' Creed. As Samuel John Stone's hymn "The Church's One Foundation" expresses it, the church is "elect from every nation" and is "one" over all the earth. The church is one great fellowship of love.

In communion with Jesus Christ, the great head of the church (see Col. 1:18), we pray for others in the body of Christ; we show love and care for them. Our union with Christ by faith also unites us with sisters and brothers in faith. The Bible gives us the following instruction: "I urge that supplications, prayers, intercessions, and thanksgivings be made for everyone" (1 Tim. 2:1). "Everyone" here includes the saints in the household of faith, the church.

Nathaniel Vincent focused on this when he wrote, "We are to pray for saints of all nations: Prayer may reach them, though never so far, and the God we pray to, is acquainted with every saint in particular, throughout the universe, knows what they all want, and how to supply all their needs."

Through our churches, we can become aware of the church universal, which is spread throughout different countries and cultures. We should "pray for saints of all nations"—for the mission and ministries of these churches, their leaders, and their congregations. No matter how far away other believers are, our prayers are important as God continues to work within churches and meet personal needs around the world.

PRAYER POINT: Gather information about the ministries of churches worldwide, and spend time praying for the needs of those who serve Christ throughout the world.

WITH HOLY ARDOR AND DESIRE

Hebrews 4:14–16

W E know that sometimes we are timid in our prayers. We do not approach God with confidence, knowing that God wants to hear us. We lack boldness and assurance.

If this describes us, we should pray for God's Spirit to energize us and remember the following instruction: "Let us therefore approach the throne of grace with boldness, so that we may receive mercy and find grace to help in time of need" (Heb. 4:16). Pray for boldness and confidence to come before the triune God—Father, Son, and Holy Spirit—at "the throne of grace."

Edward Leigh wrote about this while he defined prayer. He explained, "It is not a mere calling upon God for relief . . . but an act of spiritual adoration, a coming to God by holy ardor and desire (Heb. 4.16). The happiness of the creature is expressed by God's coming to us, and the duty of the creature by coming to him. In prayer all the three persons in the Trinity are glorified, God the Father as the object, the Son as Mediator in procuring leave for us, the Holy Spirit in giving us hearts to come to God."

Do we approach the triune God with spiritual adoration, coming to God "by holy ardor and desire"? We have the greatest reason for "happiness" since God has come to us and we are enabled through prayer to come to God. In prayer we glorify God and what God has done for us in salvation and in the life of faith!

REFLECTION QUESTIONS: In your prayers, do you keep in mind God's work of salvation in the Father, Son, and Holy Spirit? Do you have "holy ardor and desire" when you pray?

THE INTERCESSION OF CHRIST IN HEAVEN

Hebrews 7:23–25

W E should pray in praise of Jesus Christ! There is much to praise, and praising Jesus Christ is one of the blessed activities in which we can participate. Jesus Christ blesses our past, our present, and our future. So praise of Jesus Christ is our highest form of worship.

Christ's ongoing work of interceding with God for our prayers is a source of unending praise. Christ "always lives to make intercession" for us (Heb. 7:25; see also Rom. 8:34). Christ's presenting our prayers to God is the highest blessing we can imagine! To know we do not pray alone but pray in the presence and with the power of Jesus Christ is the strongest motive and affirmation of prayer we can experience. As Anthony Burgess wrote, "It's good to have this friend in the court of heaven. . . . Oh the unspeakable dignity and happiness to be under Christ's intercession. If we do so much esteem the prayer of a godly man on earth . . . what then will the prayer of Christ himself do?"

After Jesus Christ's death and resurrection, God remains "for us" in him (Rom. 8:31). Jesus intercedes for us and takes our prayers seriously. There is nothing we cannot share with Christ in prayer with the full assurance that our prayers are presented to God by the One who loved us and gave himself for us (see Gal. 2:20). While we sleep at night, Christ is at work for us!

> **PRAYER POINT:** Reflect on the many things that having Jesus Christ as our intercessor in heaven means for you. Think of Christ's work in terms of the prayers you offer, and imagine them being presented to God . . . for you! Give him praise in prayer.

O GOD,

Save thy people, bless thine inheritance, rule them also, and lift them up forever. . . .

Preserve that little flock unto whom thou hast promised to give the kingdom. . . .

Unite thy people together, let them not bite and devour one another, but endeavor by all lowliness and meekness, longsuffering, and forbearing one another, in love to keep the unity of the Spirit in the bond of peace.

Make thy way known upon earth, and thy saving health among all nations. . . . Bring in those sheep that are not yet of thy fold, and cause them to hear the voice of the great Shepherd.

As the mountains are round about Jerusalem, so be thou round about thy people from henceforth and for ever. Amen.

NATHANIEL VINCENT

BENEFITS OF CHRIST COME THROUGH PRAYER

Hebrews 9:23–28

T HE book of Hebrews presents Jesus Christ as our "great high priest" (Heb. 4:14) who offered himself as the sacrifice that takes away our sin (see 9:23–28). This is a central message of the gospel: Jesus Christ died for us (see Rom. 5:8). The deepest problem in our lives—our sin—can be forgiven by accepting the death of Christ as being done "for me" (Gal. 2:20). We receive by faith the benefits of Christ's death—forgiveness and new life in Christ (see Rom. 5:1).

Christ's death on the cross and his resurrection from the dead are the key facts of Christian faith and key facts of our own lives. When we read Christ has died "to remove sin by the sacrifice of himself" (Heb. 9:26), we know we have received the greatest gift ever. Our deepest need has been met. Now, through Christ's death as we receive Christ by faith, we have a new relationship with God that is marked by peace, love, and hope (see Rom. 5:1–5). Reconciliation has come! (see Rom. 5:10).

Prayer is the means by which this salvation becomes ours. We confess our sins to God, acknowledge Jesus Christ as our Savior, confess Christ as Lord of our lives, and begin a new life in Christ! Thomas Watson summed it up when he wrote that "all the benefits of Christ's redemption are handed over to us by prayer."

Prayer begins our walk through life with God in Christ, and prayer continues as a way we express our faith through all our days!

REFLECTION QUESTION: Contemplate the breadth and depth of the sacrifice of Jesus Christ for our sins. In what ways does this motivate you to live your faith in Christ and deepen your life of prayer?

PROVIDENCE AND PROMISES

James 1:5–8

THE book of James says, "If any of you is lacking in wisdom, ask God, who gives to all generously and ungrudgingly, and it will be given you" (1:5). James refers to the wisdom that can recognize and follow the life-giving ways of God. God is the God of wisdom, and to have wisdom is to know God's will and ways. We are to ask God for this wisdom.

We are to "ask in faith, never doubting" (v. 6). The word *doubt* here points to being conflicted, having two views of the world—our view and God's view. When we pray in faith, requesting God's wisdom, God will give it.

John Preston noted that there is a "double faith required" here. He wrote, "The one is a faith in the providence of God; the other is a faith in his promise." We must believe God will lead us and guide us in the will and ways of God (providence), and we must believe in God's promises—that God is willing to give us wisdom to live as God desires. We remember the promise of Jesus: "Ask, and it will be given you; search, and you will find; knock, and the door will be opened for you" (Matt. 7:7). When we pray, God opens the door for us, in this case, the door of life lived as God wants us to live—the Christian life itself.

God is able and willing to grant us wisdom to live life according to the ways of God. Pray for God's wisdom today!

PRAYER POINT: Pray especially that you will be given the wisdom God wants you to have. Ask to know the ways of God and how God desires you to live as a disciple of Jesus Christ.

TRUE PRAYER

James 4:1–3

Taking prayer seriously means that we know that God desires us to pray and to express our needs and desires. But we do not take this to mean that we should pray without regard to what we believe God wills us to request and have. The book of James warns believers, "You ask and do not receive, because you ask wrongly, in order to spend what you get on your pleasures" (4:3). We don't ask God profligately—recklessly, wastefully, or extravagantly. If we do, it is no surprise that our prayers are not answered by God!

Edward Dering spoke about the basics of true prayer when he wrote, "It is requisite in true prayer first that we pray only to God. Secondly, that we be inwardly touched with the need of the thing we ask. Thirdly, that we ground our prayer upon God's promise."

The basics of true prayer first are to pray to God, not to any other. Second, we must truly believe in the need of what we request from God—that it is in accord with God's will. And third, our prayer should be founded on God's promise—any request is made because we believe God hears and answers our prayers.

These basics of true prayer keep us focused on what is most important in prayer. We depend on God, we seek God's will in our prayers, and we believe God mercifully gives to us. When we keep these elements in mind, our prayers will be heard and answered by our gracious God!

REFLECTION QUESTIONS: Think of the requests you make to God in your prayers. Do they align with the elements of true prayer given here? In what ways can you use these directions as you pray?

A STOCK OF PRAYER GOING FOR ME

James 5:13–18

O NE of the true blessings and joys of being in the church is being joined with other believers in the communion of saints. The blessings come through fellowship, mutual prayers, and love for one another.

Thomas Watson gave this interesting picture of the way the prayers of God's people benefit the whole church: "Thus the prayers of the saints work for good to the Body mystical. And this is no small privilege to a child of God, that he hath a constant trade of prayer driven for him. When he comes into any place, he may say, 'I have some prayer here, nay, all the world over I have a stock of prayer going for me; when I am indisposed, and out of tune, others are praying for me, who are quick and lively.' Thus the best things work for good to the people of God."

"Pray for one another" says James (5:16). Prayers for the church benefit the church, which includes us. Watson said that when we come to any town, we can believe people are praying for us there—although they may not know our names! This is true "all the world over." Anywhere I am, "I have a stock of prayer going for me." An older meaning of the word *stock* is a supporting framework or structure. So we have a framework of prayer in place for us because those in the church are praying. Even when I'm "out of tune, others are praying for me." How wonderful!

> **PRAYER POINT:** Pray for the whole church of Jesus Christ, asking God to bless those who follow Christ. And thank God for the others in the church of Jesus Christ who pray for you—today and always!

The Ears of God

1 Peter 3:8–12

DOES God hear our prayers? At times, all of us have wondered about this. Over and over the Scriptures affirm that the answer is yes, God does hear our prayers. Yes, God answers our prayers. God's "ears are open" to our prayers (1 Peter 3:12). This is our hope, and that hope is fulfilled. Thankfully, we have experience with God hearing and answering our prayers, and this fuels our ongoing hope and confidence.

Edward Leigh strengthened us in this conviction when he wrote, "Though our prayers be weak, yet let us remember, that the promise is made to all. . . . God is more ready to hear, than we to ask, to give than we to receive. . . . His ears are open, as a kind mother or nurse who is used to being so wakeful, that she will hear the child so soon as ever it begins to cry. . . . God has specially bound himself to hear his children in those prayers, that they make unto him in their afflictions; the time of trouble is the very set hour of audience."

We need to believe God is more ready to hear than we are to ask. We need to remember the ears of God are always open. God has no difficulty in hearing us. We can be sure of this. God's nature is to be as a "kind mother or nurse" who is always "wakeful"—God will "neither slumber nor sleep" (Ps. 121:4). God hears us as soon as we begin to cry to the Lord!

> **REFLECTION QUESTIONS:** Think about times when it has seemed God has not heard your prayer. What was your reaction? What encouragements have you had that "the ears of God" are always open?

A Heart Fit for Prayer

1 Peter 4:7–11

Sometimes we may not feel in the mood to pray. For whatever reasons, we are not drawn to prayer at times. Though we know it is important, we just don't have a desire to pray.

This is understandable. But it is important for us, as much as possible, to keep constant readiness to approach the Lord. Even when we don't feel naturally inclined to pray at a certain time, we should stir ourselves to "be serious and discipline yourselves for the sake of your prayers" (1 Peter 4:7). Or, as the King James Version puts it, "watch unto prayer."

If we are always to pray to God, Thomas Manton reminded his readers, "then there must be an endeavor to keep up our hearts still in a praying temper, or in a disposition to go to God upon all occasions, that when God offers these occasions, there may not want a suitable frame of heart. The disposition and temper of heart fit for prayer must never be lost. . . . It is a difficult thing to keep up this praying frame, yet this must be a Christian's constant work and care. The whole spiritual life is but a watching unto prayer."

We must always be ready to pray. Alert, watchful, and anticipatory—these are attitudes to have so that we are immediately ready to see God at work among us and to approach God in prayers of thankfulness or petition. To "watch unto prayer" is to maintain a heart fit for prayer.

Reflection Questions: In what ways can you maintain "a heart fit for prayer"? What are ways you can move into prayer, even when you do not feel like praying?

What God Wishes to Grant

1 John 5:14–17

OUR prayer requests emerge at different times and places and for different reasons. When some situations arise, we think, *I should pray about this.* Then we may pray.

How should we decide whether or not to pray for something? We have many desires, and we believe God wants us to share our desires in prayer. But not all our desires are the same. Some are more in line with what we can believe God wants. Prayers for pure self-aggrandizement—or as some today call it a "prosperity gospel," in which people are told God always wants them to be physically and financially blessed—are not the best prayers.

We always need to remember that our prayers should be offered in relation to what we believe God truly wants for us. As the Scripture says, "This is the boldness we have in him, that if we ask anything according to his will, he hears us" (1 John 5:14). Or, as William Ames put it, "we pray to him in order to obtain by our prayer what we believe he wishes to grant." We should pray for what we believe and understand to be the will of God, what God wishes to give.

Thus, we should always keep checking our thoughts and desires in relation to our primary question: "Is this what God desires and can bless?"

REFLECTION QUESTIONS: Do you think of your prayers and petitions to God in relation to what God's will may be? In what ways can you keep focused on and close to God's will?

O GOD of hope . . .

Strengthen my weak faith, to see more clearly within the vail, that so I may be strong in hope, to enjoy, what yet I see not: and make me more acquainted, with the secrets of thy special providence, that by my own experience of thy wonderful dealing, in bringing contraries out of contraries, even light out of darkness, I may hope for the accomplishment of thy promises, though never so impossible to human capacity.

Let my hope be patient, that I may wait for that I yet enjoy not, and purify my hope daily, in the expectation of what I shall be, that so I may be purged and fitted to the enjoying thereof: season my hope with joy, that I may not quaile [sink in dejection] in any present troubles. . . .

O let me have hope even in death, because I have hope in the resurrection from the dead. And let the hope of what I enjoy not, humble me daily in the sense of my imperfections, which are the cause thereof, that so I may daily fear, and depart from evil.

Grant me these things (O God of my hope) even for thy dear Son Jesus Christ's sake, the hope of mine endless glory, to whom with thee (O righteous Father) with God the blessed Spirit the Comforter, be ascribed all glory, power, dominion, and thanksgiving for ever and ever, Amen.

EDWARD DERING

Index of Quotations

All works were written by the author whose name appears in bold above them.

Alsop, Vincent

35   *Decus & Tutamen, or, Practical Godliness* (London, 1696), 46–47.

Ames, William

25   *The Marrow of Sacred Divinity* (London, 1643), 246.

118   *The Marrow of Theology*, trans. and ed. John D. Eusden (Boston: Pilgrim Press, 1968), 260. Cf. William Ames, *The Marrow of Sacred Divinity* (London, 1643), 246.

Baxter, Richard

46   *The Crucifying of the World by the Cross of Christ* (London, 1658), 160.

56   *A Christian Directory* (London, 1673), 330.

61   *Directory*, 913.

86   *Directory*, 21.

Bayly, Lewis

20   *The Practice of Piety* (London, 1719), 157–58.

27   *Piety*, 182.

Baynes, Paul

37   *Briefe Directions Unto a Godly Life* (London, 1637), 158.

65   *The Spirituall Armour* (London, 1620), 280–81.

100   *Armour,* 270.

Bolton, Robert

34   *Certaine Devout Prayers of Mr. Bolton upon solemne occasions* (London, 1638), 122.

41   *Prayers,* 137–38.

Brooks, Thomas

39   *The Mute Christian under the Smarting Rod* (London, 1669), 326.

Bunyan, John

66   "Mr. John Bunyan's Dying Sayings," in *The Entire Works of John Bunyan,* ed. Henry Stebbing (London, 1862), 4:494.

Burgess, Anthony

74   "Sermon 25," in *CXLV Expository Sermons upon the whole 17th Chapter of The Gospel According to St. John* (London, 1656), 139–40.

82   "Sermon 41," in *Sermons,* 231.

92   "Sermon 2," in *Sermons,* 12.

110   "Sermon 2," in *Sermons,* 8.

Dent, Arthur

31   *A Learned and Fruitful Exposition vpon the Lords Prayer* (London, 1612), unnumbered.

69   *The Plaine Mans Path-way to Heaven* (London, 1684), unnumbered.

Dering, Edward

55   *Godly Private Prayers* (London, 1624), 240–43.

114   *A briefe & necessary instruction verye needefull to bee knowen of all housholders* (London, 1572), unnumbered.

119   *His Godly Priuate Prayers for Christian Families* (London, 1624), 322–29.

Dickson, David

33   *A Brief Explication of the First Fifty Psalms* (London, 1653), 211.

40   *First Fifty Psalms,* 347.

43   *A Brief Explication of the Other Fifty Psalms, From Ps. 50 to Ps. 100* (London, 1653), 23.

Downame, John

53   *A Guide to Godlynesse, or a Treatise on a Christian Life* (London, 1629), 217.

89   *Godlynesse*, 211.

Flavel, John

23   *Divine Conduct, or the Mysterie of Providence Opened in a Treatise on Psalm 57:2* (London, 1681), 104.

68   *An Exposition of the Assemblies Catechism, with Practical Inferences from Each Question* (London, 1692), 224.

Goodwin, Thomas

24   *The Returne of Prayers* (London, 1659), 104, 105.

51   *Returne*, 15–16.

58   *Returne*, 108.

87   *Returne*, 101.

102   *Returne*, 60–61.

103   *Returne*, 124.

Gouge, Thomas

57   *Christian Directions, Shewing How to Walk with God All the Day Long* (London, 1661), 23.

73   *Directions*, 14.

94   *Directions*, 26

Gouge, William

70   *A Guide to Goe to God or An Explanation of the Perfect Patterne of Prayer, the Lords Prayer* (London, 1626), 5.

91   *Guide*, 28.

95   *Guide*, 21.

Greenham, Richard

80   "A Short Forme of Catechising," in *The Workes of the Reverend and Faithfvll Servant of Jesus Christ M. Richard Greenham* (London, 1612), 91.

Gurnall, William

21   *The Christian in Complet Armour*, 5th ed. (London, 1669), 198.

44   *Armour*, 197.

Hall, Thomas

29   *An Exposition by way of Supplement, on the Fourth, fifth, sixth, seventh, eighth and ninth Chapters of the Prophecy of Amos* (London, 1661), 378.

30   *Exposition*, 378.

Henry, Matthew

26   "Directions for Daily Communion with God," in *The Complete Works of the Rev. Matthew Henry* (Edinburgh, 1853), 1:235–36.

48   "A Method for Prayer" in *Works*, 2:7–9.

59   "Directions," in *Works*, 1:216.

62   "Method," in *Works*, 2:9–10.

Hildersham, Arthur

28   *CVIII lectures upon the fourth of Iohn* (London, 1632), 219.

36   *CLII Lectures upon Psalme LI* (London, 1635), 80.

42   *Psalme LI*, 85.

Hill, Robert

96   *The Pathway to Prayer and Pietie* (London, 1613), 111.

Hopkins, Ezekiel

45   *An Exposition of the Lord's Prayer* (London, 1692), 4.

67   *Exposition*, 18.

71   *Exposition*, 53.

Leigh, Edward

64   *A Treatise of the Divine Promises* (London, 1657), 346.

84   *A Systeme or Body of Divinity* (London, 1662), 843.

109   *Systeme*, 843.

116   *Treatise*, 350–51.

Lyford, William

63   *Principles of Faith and Good Conscience* (Oxford, 1650), 217.

72   *Principles*, 229.

Manton, Thomas

106   "Sermon on 1 Thess. 5:17," in *The Complete Works of Thomas Manton* (London, 1874), 17:499–500.

117   "Sermon," in *Complete Works*, 17:501–2.

Owen, John

75   *Phronēma tou pneumatou, or, The Grace and Duty of Being Spiritually-minded Declared and Practically Improved* (London, 1681), 42.

99   *A Discourse of the Work of the Holy Spirit in Prayer*, in *The Works of John Owen, D.D.*, ed. William H. Goold (Philadelphia, 1862), 4:319.

Perkins, William

76   *Deaths Knell: or, The sicke mans Passing-Bell*, 9th ed. (London, 1628), unnumbered.

83   *Knell*, unnumbered.

98   Commentary on Galatians 4:4, in *A Commentarie upon the Epistle to the Galatians* (London, 1617), 244.

105   *A Graine of Musterd-seede*, in *The Workes of That Famovs and Worthy Minister of Christ, in the Vniversitie of Cambridge, Mr. William Perkins* (London, 1616), 1:643.

Preston, John

22   *The Saints Daily Exercise* (London, 1634), 98.

113   *Exercise*, 106.

Reynolds, Edward

50   *The Meanes and Method of Healing in the Church* (London, 1660), 35.

Scougal, Henry

90   *The Life of God in the Soul of Man* (London, 1677), 35–37.

104   *Life*, 64–65.

Scudder, Henry

81   *The Christians Daily Walk in Holy Security and Peace* (London, 1652), 629–30.

Sibbes, Richard

38   *The Brvised Reede, and Smoaking Flax* (London, 1630), 133.

79   *Reede*, 136.

93   Commentary on 2 Corinthians 1:11, in *A Learned Commentary or Exposition Upon the first Chapter of the Second Epistle of S. Paul to the Corinthians* (London, 1655), 196.

Taylor, Thomas

54   *The Principles of Christian Practice* (London, 1635), 420.

85   *Peter His Repentance Shewing* (London, 1653), 68.

101   *The Parable of the Sower and of the Seed* (London, 1621), 187.

Udall, John

32   *A Commentarie upon the Lamentations of Jeremy* (London, 1593), 136.

60   *Commentarie*, 135.

Vincent, Nathaniel

49   *The Spirit of Prayer* (London, 1674), 126.

52   *Prayer*, 118.

78   *Prayer*, 84.

88   *Prayer*, 107.

97   *Prayer*, 158, 159, 163.

108   *Prayer*, 132.

111   *Prayer*, 169–71.

Watson, Thomas

47   *A Body of Practical Divinity* (London, 1692), 424.

77   *Body*, 536.

107   *Body*, 541.

112   *Body*, 424.

115   *A Divine Cordial* (London, 1678), 22–23.

Writers

Vincent Alsop (1630–1703) was a nonconformist preacher who was active as a polemicist.

William Ames (1576–1633) was a major Puritan theologian who was exiled from Cambridge to The Netherlands where he taught the rest of his life. His *Medulla theologiae* (*The Marrow of Sacred Divinity*) became the major textbook of New England Puritans.

Richard Baxter (1615–1691) was an English Puritan church leader, poet, hymnodist, theologian, and controversialist who was ejected from the Church of England and became a nonconformist pastor.

Lewis Bayly (ca. 1575–1631) was a Calvinist who was Bishop of Bangor but emphasized Puritan-like piety and wrote the classic *The Practice of Piety*.

Paul Baynes (ca. 1573–1617) was a student of William Perkins and his successor at Great St. Andrews church. He lost his position and became an excellent casuist who influenced later Puritan theologians.

Robert Bolton (1572–1631) was a noted preacher, scholar, and pastor, known for his spiritual counseling.

Thomas Brooks (1608–1680) was a Congregationalist in church government, who was ejected from his living but continued to preach.

John Bunyan (1628–1688) was a former tinker who became a Nonconformist preacher, was imprisoned, and wrote the great Christian allegory, *The Pilgrim's Progress*.

Anthony Burgess (d. 1664) was a member of the Westminster Assembly known for being astute and pious. As a nonconformist scholar, he wrote a number of theological works.

Arthur Dent (1553–1607) was known as a great preacher whose sermons were extensively published.

Edward Dering (ca. 1540–1576) was a very learned scholar who espoused Puritan views and was well-respected by his colleagues.

David Dickson (ca. 1583–1662) was a Scots theologian and professor who was a zealous Presbyterian and opposed episcopacy in church government.

John Downame (1571–1652) was a Puritan theologian and writer who helped develop a Puritan theology of godliness and practical divinity.

John Flavel (1628–1691) was a Presbyterian and Puritan who was ejected in the Act of Uniformity but continued to preach and write numerous books. His *The Mystery of Providence* is especially notable.

Thomas Goodwin (1600–1679) was an important leader of Nonconformists, writer, and member of the Westminster Assembly. He was a Puritan "plain style" preacher and helped draft the Savoy Declaration, for Independent churches.

Thomas Gouge (1605–1681) was a son of William Gouge and a Presbyterian clergyman who was ejected for Nonconformity. He spent years in evangelism and performing acts of charity.

William Gouge (1575–1653) was a Puritan minister and author who was a member of the Westminster Assembly. He wrote a number of books and was an influential minister.

Richard Greenham (ca. 1542–1594) was an influential preacher in the development of Puritanism, known for his casuistry and spiritual counseling and his emphasis on maintaining a holy Sabbath.

William Gurnall (1616–1679) was an author and minister who embraced Puritan doctrine but maintained a ministry in the Church of England.

Thomas Hall (1610–1665) was a "high Presbyterian" who was a fervent preacher and lover of learning.

Matthew Henry (1662–1714) was a well-known biblical commentator and Nonconformist minister. His commentary on the Bible covered all the books and he wrote thirty additional works, most on practical piety.

Arthur Hildersham (1563–1632) became a Puritan and was often disciplined for his views. He lectured extensively and preached long series of sermons on Psalm 51 and the Gospel of John.

Robert Hill (d. 1623) was a Puritan minister, a writer of books on piety, and a translator of British and continental Reformed theologians.

Ezekiel Hopkins (1634–1690) maintained a position in the Church of England while writing works that strongly convey a sense of Puritan piety in clear, personal, and experiential ways.

Edward Leigh (1602–1671) was a lay member of the Long Parliament and the Westminster Assembly. He studied divinity and wrote a number of theological treatises.

William Lyford (1597–1653) was a strong Calvinist and catechizer whose writings convey Puritan piety.

Thomas Manton (1620–1677) was a Puritan Presbyterian minister, a clerk of the Westminster Assembly, and a chaplain to Oliver Cromwell. He was regarded as an excellent preacher.

John Owen (1616–1683) was a proponent of Congregationalism. He became a chaplain to Oliver Cromwell and then Dean of Christ Church College, Oxford. He wrote massively on doctrinal, practical, and controversial topics.

William Perkins (1558–1602) was a leading theologian who tremendously influenced Puritan theology as a professor at Christ's College, Cambridge and preacher at Great St. Andrew's Church. He worked to purify the established church from within. He helped mold the piety of the nation and his published works continued his influence throughout England and New England.

John Preston (1587–1628) was an influential politician, teacher, theologian, and preacher who emphasized the spiritual life. A number of his sermons were published after his death.

Edward Reynolds (1599–1676) was a member of the Westminster Assembly and later vice-chancellor of the University of Oxford and also Bishop of Norwich. He sought reconciliation among the religious parties. He wrote more than thirty books.

Henry Scougal (1650–1678) was a professor of divinity in King's College, Aberdeen, Scotland. His theological works convey depth, Christian experience, and warm piety.

Henry Scudder (ca. 1585–1662) was a member of the Westminster Assembly. His most influential work was *The Christian's Daily Walk*.

Richard Sibbes (1577–1635) was an Anglican theologian who was a "mainline Puritan" in his emphases, spiritual preaching, and friendship and influence with those in the developing Puritan movement.

Thomas Taylor (1576–1632) was a disciple of William Perkins and strongly anti-Roman Catholic and anti-Arminian. He was instrumental in training young Puritan preachers after being silenced and living with the help of patrons.

John Udall (1560?–1592) was an Anglican minister, who became associated with attacks on English bishops (Marprelate Tracts). He was imprisoned and later pardoned by the Queen before his death.

Nathaniel Vincent (1638–1677) was a Presbyterian Nonconformist minister who wrote most of his fourteen books during multiple imprisonments. He conveyed a warm and experiential piety coupled with a strong love for the church.

Thomas Watson (ca. 1620–1686) was a Presbyterian who was ejected under the Act of Uniformity (1662) but continued to preach privately until he obtained a license to preach again. His many books show doctrinal depth, strong spirituality, and extensive application and illustrations for the Christian life.

Selected Resources for Further Reflection

Beeke, Joel R., and Mark Jones. *A Puritan Theology: Doctrine for Life*. Grand Rapids: Reformation Heritage Books, 2012.

Beeke, Joel R., and Randall J. Pederson. *Meet the Puritans: With a Guide to Modern Reprints*. Grand Rapids: Reformation Heritage Books, 2006.

Collinson, Patrick. *The Elizabethan Puritan Movement*. Reprint, London: Jonathan Cape, 1971.

Haller, William. *The Rise of Puritanism*. Reprint, Philadelphia: University of Pennsylvania Press, 1972.

Haykin, Michael A. G., and Paul M. Smalley, eds. *Puritan Piety: Writings in Honor of Joel R. Beeke*. Fearn, Ross-shire, UK: Christian Focus Publications, 2018.

Kapic, Kelly M., and Randall C. Gleason, eds. *The Devoted Life: An Invitation to the Puritan Classics*. Downers Grove, IL: InterVarsity Press, 2004.

Nuttall, Geoffrey F. *The Holy Spirit in Puritan Faith and Experience*. Chicago: The University of Chicago Press, 1992.

Paul, Robert S. "The Accidence and The Essence of Puritan Piety," *Austin Seminary Bulletin: Faculty Edition*. May, 1978.

Did you enjoy this book?
Consider writing a review online.
The author appreciates your feedback!

Or write to P&R at editorial@prpbooks.com
with your comments. We'd love to hear from you.